2/85

The New Madrid Earthquakes

So great was the tumult, confusion, and groans,
Such horrors arose from the clashing of stones.

Henry Rowe Schoolcraft

The New Madrid Earthquakes

Revised Edition

James Lal Penick, Jr.

University of Missouri Press
Columbia & London
1981

Library of Congress Cataloging in Publication Data
Penick, James L.
    The New Madrid Earthquakes.
    Previously published as: The New Madrid earthquakes
of 1811–1812. 1976.
    Bibliography: p. 155
    Includes index.
    1. New Madrid (Mo.)—Earthquake, 1811.
2. New Madrid (Mo.)—Earthquake, 1812. I. Title.
QE535.2.U6P46   1981   977.8′985   81–50531
ISBN 0–8262–0344–2   AACR2

Dedicated to the Mississippi River

in appreciation of many pleasurable summer days spent afloat on its fickle surface; even in these days of marked channels, wing dams, locks, and army engineers, still a moody, uncertain, always fascinating companion.

Acknowledgments

A number of persons have cheerfully given assistance in the prosecution of this work, too many to list individually. A few were too important to ignore. Judy Washburn of the Cudahy Library, Loyola University of Chicago, maintained a steady flow of material on interlibrary loan. There were many other helpful librarians and archivists (especially at the Newberry Library); many, as is characteristic of their trade, unfortunately remain anonymous. Deserving of special mention are Frances Stadler, archivist of the Missouri Historical Society, St. Louis, and James O'Neill and Frank Burke of the National Archives and Records Service. My research assistants, Karen Hollinger, and Linda Zeagler, combed the libraries of the Chicago area for obscure narratives; Darrell Steinberg assisted in checking the accuracy of footnotes. The Committee on Research of Loyola University, chaired by that estimable graduate dean, Raymond Mariella, provided me with financial support. Donald Roll, director of the Loyola University seismology station, was very helpful in the early stages of this study. A fellow historian, Robert McCluggage, read the manuscript and in his role of department chairman provided student assistance and adjusted teaching schedules to allow time for writing. Otto Nuttli, a seismologist at Saint Louis University and a leading authority on the earthquakes, gave freely of his own research in order to assist my own, despite the fact that we have never met. He also read the finished manuscript; his courteous suggestions have saved me from several egregious errors. Any that remain are my own fault.

I have another cause for gratitude, in a class by itself.

Acknowledgments

When I was at my wit's end for a closing paragraph my daughter Katherine and wife Barbara, both devoted admirers of Louisa May Alcott, mercifully materialized a quote from *Jo's Boys*.

Foreword
by Otto W. Nuttli

The winter of 1811–1812 was a noteworthy period in the earthquake history of the United States. In mid-December, the New Madrid fault, located at the western fringe of the young country, suddenly began to release strain energy that was stored for centuries in the rock mass of the earth's crust. Thousands of earthquakes resulted, some of which were felt throughout all the existing states and as far away as Quebec City, Canada. From December through February, there were three great earthquakes, each of magnitude exceeding 8. These and fifteen of the largest aftershocks were perceptible as far as Washington, D.C., approximately 750 miles away.

Had these earthquakes occurred in the twentieth century, the Mississippi Valley would have been swarming with scientists and with representatives of the news media. However, communications were primitive in the early nineteenth century, the principal means of transportation being boat and horseback or horse-drawn vehicles. It took days for the inhabitants of the Atlantic coastal states to learn that the ground shaking they experienced had its source in the Mississippi Valley, and even longer for them to learn of the severity and extent of the earthquake damage. By this time, the earthquakes had lost some of their news value, particularly because such important matters as the affairs leading to the War of 1812 were of much more concern to the people. Thus it required a skilled historian to search through the fragmentary documents that remain and to reconstruct the response of the citizens to the awesome earthquakes. Professor Penick has succeeded admira-

Foreword

bly in this task, as the reader will discover. Not only does he portray the natural phenomena associated with the earthquake, he in addition describes the response of the small number of settlers residing in the epicentral area and of the unlucky occupants of boats on the Mississippi River at the time of the earthquakes. Also, he makes a scientific contribution in explaining the accounts of the river running backward, which was the result of damming of the river caused by vertical fault displacement of its bed.

In the early nineteenth century, the United States was too young and too poor to afford the luxury of professional scientists. Although a few amateur scientists visited the New Madrid area in the years following the earthquake, none undertook a study of the scope necessary to make a true scientific contribution. The first professional study, carried out by Myron Fuller of the United States Geological Survey, was published in 1912, one hundred years after the earthquake. Although Fuller found evidence of the severity of the earthquakes and their effects on the landscape, much important information undoubtedly was lost in the passage of a century.

The first seismograph was constructed in about 1870. The science of seismology as it is known today had its beginnings in the 1890s. Thus unfortunately there were no seismographs in existence to record the 1811–1812 sequence of earthquakes, for they would have provided the kind of data that was needed to understand the geologic forces acting in the area, forces that resulted in enormously large earthquakes for the interior of a continent. As it is, seismologists, not unlike historians, must piece together all the existing information about the 1811–1812 earthquakes, together with what they learn from the continually occurring smaller earthquakes in the area, in order to explain these phenomena. The interest not only is academic, although that of itself would be adequate justification for such studies, but there are also practical applications. For example, a knowledge of the severity of ground shaking at a particular site caused by future large earthquakes is required for safe and cost-effective design of structures. Also, disaster relief organizations need to know what to expect when great earthquakes recur, so that they can make recovery plans. This is a very important matter, for our present sophisticated technology and high population density make us much more vulnerable to earthquakes than the early settlers, who did not have and did not depend upon electrical power, energy-powered vehicles, electronic means of communication, water, natural gas and sewer lines, highways, airports, and computer systems, all of which may become inoperable or nonusable over a wide area of the mid-continent after a great earthquake. The next such earthquake will tax the resources and economy of a great portion of the central Mississippi Valley region.

Preface to the Revised Edition

The threat of major earthquakes is ever present in California. Preparation for disaster is woefully inadequate, yet residents there are psychologically prepared in the sense that virtually everyone acknowledges its likelihood, and at least the wisdom of contingency planning is recognized. By comparison, people in the Mississippi Valley are downright complacent.

Tremors are regularly recorded in the Memphis and St. Louis area and elsewhere in the central Mississippi Valley, but most can be detected only with the aid of instruments. This has resulted in a false sense of security; there is a universal human tendency to assume everything is under control until events prove otherwise. The sense of security is false because earthquakes strike suddenly and often give no warning of their approach, and because the heart of the Mississippi Valley was the scene of the most devastating earthquakes in the nation's history 170 years ago.

Recent research has shown that major quakes occur in this region on an average of every six hundred years. There is a 7 percent chance that a major quake will occur in any fifty-year period. These figures would be comforting if earthquakes obeyed the law of averages. They do not. Twelve million people now reside in the area that suffered the greatest damage during the 1811– 1812 shocks. There is no question that the onset of another series of equal magnitude would have devastating consequences. Destruction of dwellings, churches, schools, and factories, and widespread injury and death must be assumed. Little or no attention was given to earthquake resistance when existing buildings were raised; 90 percent of the casualties in a major quake would result from their collapse. *Major* is a descriptive term reserved for quakes with surface wave magnitudes of 6.5 or more, but quakes of lesser magnitude can result in structural damage and loss of life; in any fifty-year period there is a 50 percent chance that a "minor" earthquake of this character will occur.

After the San Fernando earthquake of 1971, which took sixty-four lives and destroyed property valued at a billion dollars, the Office of Emergency Preparedness attempted to initiate programs of contingency planning for the ten urban areas believed to be most in danger. Memphis–St. Louis was on that list, but at first little was accomplished. In recent years prospects have improved. There is a much better understanding today of the extent to which the region stands at risk. After the passage of the Earthquake Hazards Reduction Act by Congress in 1977, an influential report by the president's Office of Science and Technology Policy called for improved planning in six regions, including the Mississippi Valley. More importantly, money was appropriated, some of which has gone into research. Work sponsored by the United States Geological Survey, the National Science Foundation, the U.S. Nuclear Regulatory Commission, and Saint Louis University has resulted in significant breakthroughs toward a better understanding of the physical causes of earthquakes in the region. This in itself will doubtlessly quicken interest in contingency planning.

Renewed public interest in the potential hazards of the region and significant new research are sufficient reasons for issuing a revised edition of this book, in a format more generally available. An effort was made to incorporate the present state of the science in the concluding chapter. For the rest, some new material has been included, the literature updated, a few errors removed, and the prose combed through once again.

Preface to Revised Edition

I cannot close without acknowledging my debt to Prof. Otto W. Nuttli. He read part of the manuscript again and pointed out items in the scientific literature that have appeared since the first publication of this book that I would otherwise have missed. He also rescued me from several alarming mistakes; needless to say, any that remain are my responsibility. I am very grateful.

James Lal Penick, Jr.
Loyola University of Chicago
April 1981

Preface to the First Edition

The earthquake descriptions that appeared in newspapers and elsewhere are the sources for this study. They represent a surprising variety of humanity—male and female, educated and ignorant, preachers and sinners, as well as scientists, poets, rivermen, merchants, Indians, and an undifferentiated assortment. The earthquakes were a great equalizer. When it would not interrupt the flow of the narrative these voices are allowed to speak for themselves. Many seem haunted by their brush with one of the most terrifying forces nature can unleash, as if reminded too brusquely of their mortality. But a surprising number were careful and meticulous observers in the midst of great stress. That terrible curiosity, that insatiable desire to catalog and describe that in Western nations has produced the fearsome structure called science, was very much in evidence in both its rudimentary and sophisticated forms. Apparently, if Americans are suddenly introduced into a situation in which the ground shakes for weeks and months on end and all nature seems about to come undone, the first impulse of many is to count, make lists, and sort. Seen in that light this study is the latest stage in a response begun 164 years ago.

James Lal Penick, Jr.
January 1976

Contents

1. The Shocks Begin, 1

An Eventful Voyage: The experience of John Bradbury, twenty miles east of the epicenter—*The Earthquakes and the Nation*—Their impact nationally—*The Signs of the Times:* The earthquakes, comet, wars and rumors of wars considered portents.

2. New Madrid, 15

Origins in the Spanish Conspiracy; the vision of George Morgan; history of the town before the earthquake—*The Sixteenth of December:* Effect on the town of the earthquakes; the accounts in the narratives; damage minimal; epicenter sixty-five miles to southwest—*Little Prairie:* Closer to epicenter, destruction was greater—*The Seventh of February:* Epicenter now closer to New Madrid; destruction of the town, and flight—*The Aftermath:* Land frauds; decline of the district.

3. The Mississippi River, 52

The Sixteenth of December: Impact on the river, a major avenue of commerce; onslaught of the shocks; falling of the banks; ubiquitous agitation of water's surface; the narratives and the river's sudden rise and plunge; disturbance of the bed; the rising of the trees; the sinking of the islands—*The Seventh of February:* Why no good accounts exist of 23 January; experience of Vincent Nolte; rising of the bed and reversal of the current; scientific skepticism; consideration of the evidence—

1. The Shocks Begin

The extent of territory which has been shaken, nearly at the same time, is astonishing—reaching on the Atlantic coast from Connecticut to Georgia and from the shores of the ocean inland to the State of Ohio. . . . In North Carolina a volcano has appeared, and . . . in an eruption a few days since, a flood of lava poured out which ran to the distance of three quarters of a mile. *The period* is portentous and alarming. We have within a few years seen the most wonderful eclipses, the year past has produced a magnificent comet, the earthquakes within the past two months have been almost without number—and in addition to the whole, we constantly *"hear of wars and summons of wars."* May not the same enquiry be made of us that was made by the hypocrites of old—"Can ye not discern the signs of the times."

Pittsburgh Gazette, 10 April 1812
from the *Connecticut Mirror*

The earthquakes began about two o'clock on the morning of Monday, 16 December 1811. The time of this and of all successive shocks (called "shakes" in the west, "rockings" in the southeast) was somewhat imprecise. Not a single exact reckoning was fixed for any shock in any part of the country. "Some time-pieces [were] set to solar, and others to mean time," said one impatient observer, "and . . . most of them [were] inaccurate."[1] Still, there was general agreement on every shock within a range of twenty or thirty minutes.

1. Daniel Drake, *Natural and Statistical View or Picture of Cincinnati and the Miami Country* (Cincinnati: Looker and Wallace, 1815), p. 238.

1

The New Madrid Earthquakes

One of the most vivid descriptions of the onset of the shakes was left by a scientist. John Bradbury was a Scottish naturalist commissioned by the Botanical Society of Liverpool to study and collect specimens of North American plant life. In December 1811 he was embarked on the Mississippi for New Orleans; he had lately returned to St. Louis from a long trip up the Missouri as far as the Mandan villages, two thousand miles from the river's mouth. On the fourteenth he left New Madrid, a town on the Mississippi seventy miles below the junction of the Ohio, and the following evening arrived in the vicinity of the second Chickasaw Bluff, one hundred miles downstream. This was just north of island number thirty-six and a channel reputed to be the most treacherous on the river, appropriately called the Devil's Race Ground. It appeared to be choked with planters and sawyers.[2] The boat was more maneuverable than the clumsy Kentucky flatboats, which relied mainly on the current for propulsion. Its French crew used oars to make headway, and it had a skilled steersman aboard as well. It carried a cargo of thirty thousand pounds of lead, however, and prompted by caution they moored to a small island to await the morning rather than attempt to thread the

2. A planter was a tree with one end fixed in the river's bottom, so that it stood motionless and erect. Sometimes no more than a slight difference in the water's ripple hinted at its presence as it lay in wait to impale the boats of luckless or inattentive navigators. Sawyers were also trees with one end fixed in the bottom but were more noticeable because the surfaced end rose and fell with the current in a sawing motion. What to the inexperienced eye might seem to be a branch bobbing in the water would, when run upon, turn out to be an entire tree, braced for the impact.

Throughout this work island numbers are taken from Zadok Cramer, *The Navigator,* 8th ed. (Pittsburgh: Cramer, Spear and Eichbaum, 1814), reprinted in Ethel C. Leahy, *Who's Who on the Ohio and Its Tributaries* (Cincinnati: E. C. Leahy Publishing Co., 1931).

2

"The Great Earthquake at New Madrid"
Henry Howe, *The Great West* (Cincinnati, 1851), p. 237, in The
State Historical Society of Missouri, Columbia, Mo.

partially obstructed channel in the waning daylight hours. It was the evening of 15 December.[3]

Bradbury was awakened from a sound sleep about two in the morning by "a most tremendous noise." Before he could orient himself the boat gave a sudden unsettling lurch, as if it had been lifted from the water and dropped abruptly. Once on deck he found that the river was turbulent; although the boat was still moored, "all nature seemed running into chaos." With magnificent composure he began to unravel the confused scene. Noises mingled in the air, creating a horrid din: screaming wildfowl, the snapping and cracking of falling trees, the sound of a violent tempest of wind where there was no wind. One sound, however, dominated the others, "equal to the loudest thunder, but more hollow and vibrating." This was the noise of the earthquake, to which every eyewitness would testify. Another sound, a warning of greater danger, soon joined in the concert: the roar of vertical banks plunging into the river, starting swells that threatened to capsize the boat.[4]

They were moored to a sloping bank, which saved their lives. All along the river, boats brought to rest for the night under high banks were swamped or crushed. Their own bank gaped in a chasm eighty yards long and four feet wide. By daylight Bradbury had counted twenty-seven shocks, although none had been as hard

3. Reuben Gold Thwaites, ed., *Early Western Travels, 1748–1846*, vol. 5: *Bradbury's Travels in the Interior of America, 1809–1811* (Cleveland: Arthur H. Clark Co., 1904), pp. 9–15, 203–4, hereafter cited as *Bradbury's Travels*. Here, in an account written some years later, the Devil's Race Ground was called Devil's Channel or *Chenal du Diable*, but a narrative written by Bradbury in New Orleans soon afterward uses the correct name; see St. Louis *Louisiana Gazette*, 7 March 1812.

4. *Bradbury's Travels*, p. 204; St. Louis *Louisiana Gazette*, 7 March 1812.

as the first. The sight of the river in the morning's first light did little to reduce the apprehensions of the boatmen. Its surface was covered with foam. Entire trees were carried along with the current. Boats floated by, fully loaded, ominously without crews or passengers.[5]

As they prepared to embark a shock occurred that was nearly as severe as the first. The frighened crew abandoned ship and would probably have scattered, but a giant tree fell and blocked their path across the chasm. Bradbury saw the bank begin to give way entirely and ordered the lines cut; rather than pitch into the river with the bank the crew hastily came aboard, and they drifted out into the channel. The Devil's Race Ground came in sight. It appeared utterly impassable: A great forest of trees lodged against the planters fixed in the river's bottom. The men lost heart and refused to go on. Bradbury found a bank with a gentle slope and moored. They went ashore to prepare breakfast and calm unsettled nerves. Bradbury and the crew endured three more severe shocks during this time, but fortified with food and a ration of grog, and stiffened by pungent oratory, they set out again.

The danger we had now to encounter was of a nature which they understood: the nearer we approached it, the more confidence they appeared to gain; and indeed, all their strength, and . . . skill . . . was necessary; for there being no direct channel through the trees, we were several times under the necessity of changing our course in the space of a few seconds, and that so instantaneously, as not to leave a moment for deliberation. Immediately after we had cleared all danger, the men dropped their oars, crossed themselves, then gave a shout, which was followed by mutual congratulations on their safety.[6]

The earthquake's center usually has been identified

5. *Bradbury's Travels*, p. 206.
6. Ibid., pp. 207–8.

with New Madrid. The little village was devastated, but the epicenter of the first series of shocks was about sixty-five miles to the southwest in northeastern Arkansas, twenty miles due west of the point where Bradbury moored for the night. The earthquakes, however, were a national event. Over a period of months shocks were felt in the southeast, in the middle seaboard states, in New England, in Detroit, in Canada's Province of Quebec, far up the Missouri River, and in New Orleans. The area within which tremors could be felt without the aid of instruments approached one million square miles.[7]

The number of shocks and the length of time over which they occurred were remarkable. Many people kept a count; only one had the stamina to last the duration. Jared Brooks, a Louisville engineer and surveyor, counted a total of 1,874 shocks between 16 December and 15 March, 8 of which he classed as violent, 10 as very severe, 35 as moderate but alarming, and the rest between generally and barely perceptible. In common with many others he rigged pendulums capable of detecting the horizontal earth waves. Some of the shocks, however, seemed to pound up and down and were usually described as vertical. To detect these he devised a system of springs. Most people chose to get along without instruments. Many shocks were easily perceptible at great distances without them. Persons in Detroit and Canada, six hundred miles from the center, counted 9 by early April. From about the same distance, those living in Charleston, South Carolina,

7. Otto W. Nuttli, "The Mississippi Valley Earthquakes of 1811 and 1812: Intensities, Ground Motion and Magnitudes," *Bulletin of the Seismological Society of America* 63:1 (19 February 1973):231; Myron Fuller, "The New Madrid Earthquake," U.S. Geological Survey *Bulletin* 494 (Washington: Government Printing Office, 1912):17.

The Shocks Begin

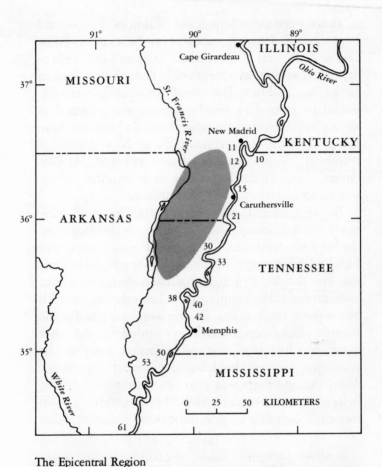

The Epicentral Region
Shaded area is the region of numerous sand blows; numbers along river refer to islands as listed in Cramer's *The Navigator;* Caruthersville was Little Prairie. Otto W. Nuttli, "The Mississippi Valley Earthquakes of 1811 and 1812," U.S. Geological Survey *Earthquake Information Bulletin* 6:2 (1974) :10.

experienced nearly as many shocks in the first two days.[8]

There were three sequences of shocks. The second began on 23 January, which many believed to be as severe as the first in December. The third on 7 February began with a shake memorable enough to be known as the "hard" shock. The initial disturbances were followed by secondary shocks, which often seemed as severe to observers as the main ones. In between these the ground shook incessantly. Near New Madrid it trembled "like the flesh of a beef just killed." At Cincinnati a pendulum hung in a front window "never ceased to vibrate in nearly five months."[9]

To some extent, but not entirely, the impression made by the earthquakes depended on distance from the center. Residents of New Orleans, some five hundred miles away on a straight line south, did not feel the first shocks, although slight trembling may have gone unnoticed by people asleep. Later shocks were felt but without much effect. People were disturbed at the theater, clocks stopped, crockery rattled. On the other hand, at Charleston, somewhat farther away to the southeast, the first shock made a distinct impression. Many thought there was a fire, so clamorously did the bells of St. Philip's steeple ring. "Houses were so much moved," according to one ponderous observer, "that

8. Henry McMurtrie, *Sketches of Louisville and Its Environs* (Louisville: S. Penn, 1819), pp. 233, 255; Fuller, "New Madrid Earthquake," pp. 22, 27–28, 32–33; *New York Evening Post*, 1 January 1812; *Pittsburgh Gazette*, 31 January 1812; Adam Walker, *A Journal of Two Campaigns of the Fourth Regiment of U.S. Infantry* (Keene, N.H.: Printed by the author, 1816), pp. 38–39; Louis Houck, *A History of Missouri*, vol. 3 (New York: Arno Press and *New York Times*, 1971), p. 175; Drake, *Natural and Statistical View*, pp. 235, 237.

9. Houck, *History of Missouri,* p. 175.

persons were induced to rise from their beds." Clocks stopped and furniture moved about unbidden. The concussion of 23 January cracked pavements and plaster. At Richmond, Washington, and Norfolk the story was much the same.[10]

Scars of the earthquake were rare far from the center, but here and there it left its mark. The first shock reportedly caused the parade ground at Georgetown, South Carolina, to sink one or two inches. A phenomenon frequently blamed on earthquakes in the past, dry wells, occurred at Columbia, South Carolina.[11]

Americans were familiar with earthquakes. One hundred and fifty-four occurred in eastern North America between 1628 and 1782. A memorable shock had damaged Boston on 18 November 1755, causing an outbreak of jeremiads among the ministers; their case had been strengthened by an earthquake earlier in the month that laid Lisbon, Portugal, in ruins. Tremors had been felt in the vicinity of Columbia, South Carolina, and Augusta, Georgia, as recently as January 1811. But the prolonged shocks that began in December were different. "We venture to say," said a report from Augusta after the series that began on 7 February, "that a large proportion of our inhabitants, never lay

10. New Orleans *Louisiana Gazette and Daily Advertiser*, 21 December 1811, 24 January 1812; St. Louis *Louisiana Gazette*, 7 March 1812; *New York Evening Post,* 31 January 1812; quote in Samuel Latham Mitchill, "A Detailed Narrative of the Earthquakes," *Transactions of the Literary and Philosophical Society of New York* 1 (1814):285.

11. *New York Evening Post*, 26 December 1811; Mitchill, "Detailed Narrative," p. 284; C. F. Volney, *A View of the Soil and Climate of the United States of America* (Philadelphia: J. Conrad and Co., 1804), pp. 97–98; Edward Darrell Smith, "On the Changes Which Have Taken Place in the Wells Situated in Columbia, S.C. since the Earthquakes of 1811–12," *American Journal of Science and Arts* 1:1 (1818):93–95.

down at night with feelings similar to those they experienced when going to bed during the past week."[12]

Also alarming was the rash of earthquakes elsewhere in the same general time period. "From the beginning of the year 1811 till 1813," wrote the scientist Edwin James, a member of Stephen Long's expedition to the Rocky Mountains,

a vast extent of the earth lying between 50° and 45° of north latitude, limited by the meridian of the Azores, the range of the Alleghanies and the Green Mountains of Vermont, the valley of the Missouri, the cordilleras of New Grenada, the coasts of Venezuela, and the Volcanoes of the smaller West India Islands, was shaken at the same time by commotions attributed to subterranean fire.[13]

While the earthquakes continued many people were led to examine the signs, to "inspect the entrails of the times," in the disgusted words of John C. Calhoun. The year 1811 had little to recommend it, in any event. May had brought more trouble at sea with Great Britain. Years of embargo and nonintercourse, of idle ships, and of goods piling up on wharves had left the merchants of the northeast impatient of the government's policy of economic sanctions and opposed to war with Great Britain over neutral rights, but people of the south and west, with eyes on Canada and the Floridas, were lively for war. The nation was divided bitterly. In November, the American army fought a great battle with the In-

12. Volney, *View of the Soil and Climate*, pp. 97–98; Philadelphia *Pennsylvania Gazette*, 1 January 1812; *New York Evening Post*, 5 March 1812. For examples of sermons evoked by the 1755 earthquakes see Charles Chauncey, *Earthquakes a token of the righteous Anger of God* (Boston, 1755); Thomas Foxcroft, *The Earthquake a Divine Visitation* (Boston, 1756); Jonathan Mayhew, *A Discourse . . . Occasioned by Earthquakes . . .* (Boston, 1755).

13. Edwin James, *Account of an Expedition from Pittsburgh to the Rocky Mountains*, vol. 65 (Ann Arbor: University Microfilms, 1966), pp. 326–27.

dians at Tippecanoe, on the banks of the Wabash. Losses on both sides were heavy, and the Shawnee leader, Tecumseh, was still at large. It was commonly known that war with Great Britain meant war with the Indians, already aided and encouraged by the governor of Canada.

On 5 November President James Madison called Congress in session a month early and recommended that the country prepare for hostilities. On the floor of the House, in the months before the declaration of war in June, John Randolph of Roanoke heaped iniquity on the war party and warned of the dire consequences it courted: "If other civilized people . . . have not escaped, what reason have we to suppose that we shall be preserved from the calamities which providence has thought fit to inflict on those nations which have ventured to intermingle in the conflicts now going on in Europe?" Calhoun replied from the same lofty heights: The nation was "roused from its lethargy . . . determined to vindicate its honor." Like the immovable object and the irresistible force, inflated eloquence met magnificent pomposity.[14]

The year's disasters began in the spring with flood waters so high in the Ohio and Mississippi valleys that men remembered it as the "year of waters." December ended with a "furious and memorable tempest" that swept the coast from Hatteras to Newfoundland and a fire in a Richmond, Virginia, theater that extinguished the lives of seventy people, among them the governor of the state. In between, the portents accumulated. In September a brilliant comet—always a sign of fore-

14. U.S., Congress, *Debates and Proceedings of the Congress of the United States*, 12th Cong., 1st sess., 4 November 1811 to 6 July 1812, 2 (Washington: Gales and Seaton, 1853): 1385, 1398– 99; Glenn Tucker, *Tecumseh: Vision of Glory* (New York: Bobbs-Merrill Co., 1956).

boding—appeared in the heavens and shone through the fall and early into the following year. Later, looking back, men sought for other signs missed at the time. Daniel Drake of Cincinnati, a physician, remembered the bilious remitting and intermittent fever of the autumn that infected the people along the Ohio and Mississippi and puzzled over strange refractions of the sun he had noted the previous spring.[15] William Leigh Pierce, a young man of twenty-one on a "tour" from Pittsburgh to New Orleans when the earthquakes occurred, described an "astonishing precursor" of the shocks.

On the 30th of November, 1811, about one half hour before sun-rise, two vast electrical columns shot up from the eastern horizon, until their heads reached the zenith; their advance and exit were rapid, and the light which they diffused was very sensible. From that time until the 16th of December, there was a continued want of perfect transparency in the atmosphere, and wherever the sun was even partially visible, it exhibited a dull and fiery redness.[16]

Within a couple of decades such recollections had sprouted into a variety of tall tales, in which even the "inhabitants of the forest" that fall were filled with restless apprehension.

A countless multitude of squirrels, obeying some great and universal impulse, which none can know but the Spirit that gave them being, left their reckless and gamboling life, and their ancient places of retreat in the north, and were seen pressing forward by tens of thousands in a deep and sober

15. Timothy Flint, *The History and Geography of the Mississippi Valley*, vol. 1 (Cincinnati: E. H. Flint and L. R. Lincoln, 1832), p. 313: Mitchill, "Detailed Narrative," p. 281. Drake, *Natural and Statistical View*, pp. 239–40; William Leigh Pierce, Esq., *The Year: A Poem in Three Cantoes* (New York: David Longworth, 1813), appendix, pp. 20–21.

16. Pierce, *The Year*, appendix, pp. 16–17. He was the son of a delegate to the Federal Constitutional Convention in 1787, also William Leigh Pierce.

The Shocks Begin

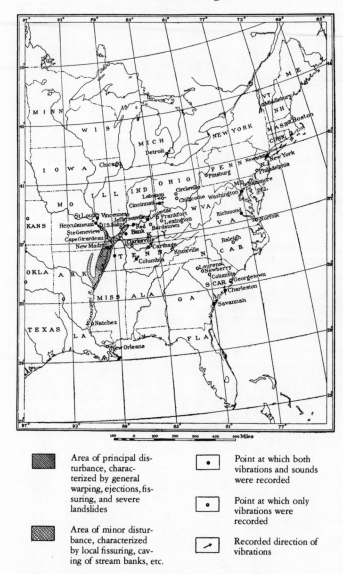

Area of principal disturbance, characterized by general warping, ejections, fissuring, and severe landslides

Area of minor disturbance, characterized by local fissuring, caving of stream banks, etc.

Point at which both vibrations and sounds were recorded

Point at which only vibrations were recorded

Recorded direction of vibrations

The Earthquakes and the Nation
Myron L. Fuller, "The New Madrid Earthquake," U.S. Geological Survey *Bulletin* 494 (Washington: Government Printing Office, 1912):8, fig. 1. Provided by The John Crerar Library, Chicago, Ill.

phalanx to the South. No obstacles seemed to check their extraordinary and concerted movement; the word had been given them to go forth, and they obeyed it, though multitudes perished in the broad Ohio, which lay in their path.[17]

Randolph predicted a "dreadful scourge—some great desolation—some awful visitation." Calhoun heaped scorn on "superstition," derided the "comets, earthquakes . . . the whole catalogue of omens" enumerated by his antagonist and labeled them all mere "physical appearances." Such references were infrequent over the long course of the debates and probably had as much to do with rhetorical excess as with susperstition. Yet the occasional turn taken by the debates seemed to prove the point: It was "a time of extraordinaries."[18]

17. Charles Joseph Latrobe, *The Rambler in North America*, vol. 1 (London: R. B. Seeley and W. Burnside, 1835), pp. 102–3.

18. *Debates and Proceedings*, pp. 1385, 1398–99; Mitchill, "Detailed Narrative," p. 300.

2. New Madrid

We have seen a statement made by a couple of gentlemen just from New Madrid, which says that that place is much torn to pieces by the late Earthquake; so much so, that it is "almost" impossible to get along in any way, but entirely so on horse-back. The houses of brick, stone and log are torn to pieces, and those of frame thrown upon their sides. The ground near that place for 100 acres has sunk so low that the tops of the tallest trees can hardly be seen above the water, in other places more than half the length of the timber is under water. The citizens have fled to the mountains, and were, when the informants left there, waiting for an opportunity to move to Kentucky. It is said that they are near one-thousand in number! Merciful God! What a horrid situation.

New York Evening Post
11 March 1812

Outside of the Mississippi Valley few people today are aware of the existence of the town of New Madrid (pronounced mad' • rəd) in Missouri's southeastern bootheel region. It was probably better known before it was "much torn to pieces." The curious circumstances surrounding its establishment and early history, as well as its once-strategic location at the gateway of the trans-Mississippi west, had made it a familiar, if not a famous, name.

New Madrid was founded by Col. George Morgan, a prominent patriot of the American Revolution. On 3 January 1789 he left Fort Pitt with seventy other Americans in four armed boats. Their destination was the Spanish territory on the western bank of the Mis-

15

sissippi, where they intended to establish a colony and become the subjects of His Catholic Majesty, the king of Spain.[1]

This idea had occurred to others. In Kentucky the Spanish policy of closing the Mississippi to Americans had brought men close to desperation. Distance and the cost of overland transport prohibited eastward trade; with no exit at the port of New Orleans, eventual strangulation seemed inevitable unless something was done. This frustration was deliberate policy. The Spanish minister to the United States, Diego de Gardoqui, had instructions to buy acquiescence in the closing of the river from Congress while working secretly to alienate westerners from their government. The Mississippi was to be used as bait to lure the population of Kentucky. Drawn by the promise of free trade on the river, Americans would form colonies in Spanish Louisiana; from the chief threat to the king's possession they would be transformed into its first line of defense.[2]

Kentuckians who looked to their government for relief were disillusioned by the revelations of the Jay-Gardoqui negotiations, which seemed to demonstrate the willingness of Congress to surrender the American demand for free navigation of the Mississippi in return for a few commercial concessions advantageous to the maritime states. Some angry Kentuckians talked of secession, while others threatened to take matters in hand and open New Orleans by force. Either course would have been disastrous for the Republic, which stood to lose a territory or gain a war. The British in Canada, whose fort at Detroit threatened the American hinter-

1. Max Savelle, *George Morgan: Colony Builder* (New York: Columbia University Press, 1932); also Savelle, "The Founding of New Madrid, Missouri," *Mississippi Valley Historical Review* 19 (June 1932): 30–56.

2. Savelle, *George Morgan*, p. 202.

SEVERAL Gentlemen, who propose to make Settlements in the Western Country, mean to reconnoitre and survey the same the ensuing Winter. All Farmers, Tradesmen, &c. of good Characters, who wish to unite in this Scheme, and to visit the Country under my Direction, shall be provided with Boats and Provisions for the Purpose, free of Expence, on signing an Agreement, which may be seen by applying to me at Prospect, near Princeton, on or before the 8th Day of October; or at Fort Pitt, by the 20th Day of November next. The Boats which will be employed on this Expedition, are proposed to be from 40 to 60 Feet long, to row with twenty Oars each, and to carry a Number of Swivels. Each Man to provide himself with a good Firelock, or Rifle, Ammunition, and one Blanket, or more if he pleases—Such as choose Tents, or other Conveniences, must provide them for themselves. Every Person who accompanies me in this Undertaking, shall be entitled to 326 Acres of Land, at one eighth of a Dollar per Acre. Those who first engage to have the Preference of Surveys; which, however, each Person may make in such Part of the whole Tract as he pleases, taking none but his Choice of the best Lands: provided each Survey is either a Square or Oblong, whose Sides are East, West, North and South: 640 Acres, or more, being first reserved for a Town, which I propose to divide into Lots of One Acre each, and give 600 of them, in Fee, to such Merchants, Tradesmen, &c. as may apply on the Spot, and 40 of them to such Public Uses as the Inhabitants shall, from Time to Time, recommend: together with one Out Lot of 10 Acres to each of the first 600 Families who shall build and settle in the Town.

All Persons who settle with me at New-Madrid, and their Posterity, will have the free Navigation of the Mississippi, and a Market at New-Orleans, free from Duties, for all the Produce of their Lands, where they may receive Payment in Mexican Dollars for their Flour, Tobacco, &c.

It is proposed, after fixing on the Spot, to clear and fence in 100 Acres, in a convenient Situation, to plant it with Corn—to hire suitable Hands to tend it through the Summer; and in the next Fall, Winter and Spring, to distribute it to all New Settlers at one eighth of a Dollar per Bushel, that they may have Dependance so far as this will go: and as Buffaloes and other Game are very plenty in the Neighbourhood, there can be no Want of Provisions, Contractors being ready to engage to deliver fresh Beef and Venison throughout the Year, at One Penny per Pound.

Credit will be given to those who desire it, as well for the Land as for Provisions, and Payment received in future Produce. All Persons will be assisted in building a House, clearing a Spot of Ground, and in getting in their first Crops. Horned Cattle, Horses, and Swine, will be delivered to the Settlers at New-Madrid in such Quantities as they stand in Need of at first, at very reasonable Rates, for Cash or future Produce.

Those who settle at New-Madrid in this or the ensuing Year, shall have Plough-Irons or other Iron-Work, and farming Utensils transported down the Ohio gratis: also their Cloathing, Bedding, kitchen Furniture, and certain other Articles which may not be too bulky.

Schoolmasters will be engaged immediately for the Instruction of Youth.—Ministers of the Gospel will meet with Encouragement: and Grants of Land made in Fee to each of every Denomination, who may agree with a Congregation before the Year 1790: beside particular Grants of Tracts of Land to each Society.

This new City is proposed to be built on a high Bank of the Mississippi River, near the Mouth of the Ohio, in the richest and most healthiest Part of the Western Country, about the Latitude of 37°.

Those who wish for further Information, will be pleased to apply to me in Person as above-mentioned, or at the New-City of Madrid, after the first Day of next December, where Surveyors will attend to lay out the Lands.

GEORGE MORGAN.

October 3, 1788.

Handbill issued by George Morgan to advertise his projected expedition to New Madrid, courtesy of The State Historical Society of Missouri, Columbia, Mo.

land, sought to exploit the situation. Their agent, Dr. John Connolly, appeared in Louisville at the end of 1788 and tried to incite an attack on New Orleans, even promising British aid. Ironically, Morgan was delayed because he uncovered Connolly's plot. He wrote reassuringly to George Washington that the people of Kentucky were attracted to neither the British Intrigue nor the Spanish Conspiracy. Yet Morgan was himself an instrument of Spain. His expedition was made possible by Gardoqui's endorsement and financial support. James Madison, who obtained one of Morgan's handbills advertising for settlers, called it "the most authentic & precise evidence of the Spanish project that has come to my knowledge."[3]

Personal disappointment had a part to play in Morgan's decision to turn his back on the United States. He was no stranger to colonizing schemes. As a member of the Indiana Company he had sought unsuccessfully for twenty years to gain title to 1.8 million acres west of the Appalachian Mountains. His hopes were dashed in 1784 when Virginia ceded its western land claims to the United States; it kept for itself the area south of the Ohio River where the Indiana lands were located. To recoup, Morgan formed the New Jersey Land Society and petitioned Congress for a large grant in Illinois. The petition was accepted in 1788, but on terms he believed to be unreasonable.[4]

It was at this point that Morgan took the bait from Gardoqui, but he was not the only prominent American to rise to it. George Rogers Clark, the conqueror of the

3. Ibid., pp. 207, 210; Gaillard Hunt, ed., *The Writings of James Madison*, vol. 5 (New York: G. P. Putnam's Sons, 1904), pp. 332–37; Dale Van Every, *Ark of Empire: The American Frontier, 1784–1803* (New York: New American Library Mentor Book, 1964), p. 142.

4. Savelle, *George Morgan*, pp. 76–110, 200–201.

George Morgan
Courtesy of The State Historical Society of Missouri, Columbia, Mo.

British post at Vincennes, whose deeds had forced the British to recognize the Mississippi as the western boundary of the United States, was bitter and resentful by 1788. In March he wrote Gardoqui offering to found a colony of Americans on the Spanish side of the river. He and Morgan held in common a belief "that no property or persons" was safe under a "government so weak and infirm as that of the United States."[5] When Morgan started down the Ohio, that government was defunct. A Constitution had been ratified creating a new one, but it had yet to be formed, and no one, in his opinion, could guarantee that it would work any better.

Morgan selected a site on the west bank of the Mississippi reaching from the mouth of the St. Francis to a point well north of the Ohio junction, encompassing 15 million acres. He chose L'Anse à la graisse,[6] seventy miles below the Ohio, for the location of his town, which—thinking to please the king, who had not yet confirmed the grant—he dubbed New Madrid. That spring he laid out the townsite and then journeyed to New Orleans to confer with the governor, Esteban Miró. But the citizen of Kentucky who did so much to frustrate Clark also foiled Morgan.

James Wilkinson, who had dislodged Clark as commanding general in the west, was a principal actor in the Spanish Conspiracy. The convolutions of his twisted scheming will never be unraveled completely, but clearly he was bent on profiting personally from the Kentucky crisis. He had managed by this time to con-

5. James Alton James, *The Life of George Rogers Clark* (Chicago: University of Chicago Press, 1928), pp. 392–93; Savelle, *George Morgan*, p. 204.

6. "Cove of grease"; so called because of the abundance of bear and buffalo meat found there. William E. Foley, *A History of Missouri*, vol. 1: *1673 to 1820* (Columbia: University of Missouri Press, 1971), p. 49.

New Madrid

vince Miró of his willingness to maneuver Kentucky into the Spanish embrace. He had also extracted a number of privileges that the New Madrid project threatened. Though an American officer, this rogue was secretly in Spanish employment as an agent to encourage an attitude favorable to Spain in Kentucky, and to illustrate the advantages of such a connection he enjoyed the exclusive privilege of marketing his goods in New Orleans. He was also the sole agent to plant American colonies on the west bank of the Mississippi. He treated Morgan as a dangerous competitor. With magnificent cheek he branded the interloper as a man governed by "the vilest self-interest" and the new colony as contrary to Spanish interests.[7]

Miró was inclined to agree. Gardoqui had allowed Morgan privileges that made the colony virtually autonomous. It was to have self-government as well as freedom of worship. Though the colonists would take an oath of allegiance to the king, they would remain American in every other respect and at the first disagreement would probably rebel. Morgan, and not a Spanish official, would be in command, with full powers of appointment and the right to sell all lands and establish schools. To Miró, this scheme was reckless in the extreme. Thus when Morgan arrived in New Orleans he found the governor adamant in his insistence on alterations in the original agreement. Only the Roman Catholic church would conduct services, although no colonist would be disturbed in his beliefs. Self-government was not to be allowed. Miró would send a garrison and commandant, although he would concede to Morgan the position of second in command.

7. James Ripley Jacobs, *Tarnished Warrior: Major-General James Wilkinson* (New York: Macmillan Co., 1938), p. 95; James, *Life of George Rogers Clark*, p. 395.

He was also commissioned to bring in more colonists but, in accord with normal Spanish policy, land was to be allotted free, not sold. As a kind of consolation prize, Morgan and each of his sons would be given a grant of one thousand acres.[8]

Denied the right to sell land, Morgan had lost his chief pecuniary interest in the colony. After his return to New Jersey, he decided to abandon the project. The new government under the Constitution and the creation of the Supreme Court apparently rekindled his hopes for a favorable decision on the Indiana grant by an impartial tribunal. He sponsored a suit against Virginia (and precipitated the crisis that led to ratification of the Eleventh Amendment), but without success; in 1796 he was angling for a large grant in Canada, once again offering to change his allegiance.[9] Another, less obvious factor may have helped to discourage his plans for New Madrid. In 1789 the Spanish reopened the Mississippi to American commercial traffic, provided a heavy duty was paid.

Whatever may be said of Morgan's scheming, he was not open to the charge of petty thinking. His plan for the colony had a breathtaking scale. Wilkinson, for instance, had advised the Spanish to keep the river closed to American traffic (in fact, he too lost interest in his Spanish connection when the river was opened).

8. Savelle, *George Morgan*, pp. 204–5, 221–22; Foley, *History of Missouri*, pp. 36–37.

9. Savelle, *George Morgan*, pp. 109–10, 226; Foley, *History of Missouri*, p. 37; see Morgan to Alexander McKee, 16 April 1796, in E. A. Cruikshank, ed., *The Correspondence of Lieutenant Governor John Graves Simcoe*, vol. 5 (Toronto: Ontario Historical Society, 1931), pp. 154–56. "The judicial power of the United States shall not be construed to extend to any suit in law or equity, commenced or prosecuted against one of the United States by citizens of another State, or by citizens or subjects of any foreign state."—Eleventh Amendment.

His plan was simplicity itself but revealed a mean willingness to exploit desperation. He advised that L'Anse à la graisse be fortified to block an invasion attempt from Kentucky while encouraging Americans to settle on the Spanish side to escape trade restrictions—with Wilkinson, of course, the agent to plant such colonies.[10]

Morgan also advised against opening the river to Americans, but for him this was the essential element in his design for a great city. The river would be closed, but Americans could bring their goods to New Madrid and pay only a small duty. His town would become the marketplace for the trade of the American interior. He even hoped that its proximity to the Osage River (150 miles inland) would enable it to capture the fur trade of the Missouri River and displace St. Louis. Morgan envisioned nothing less than a great metropolis at the gateway of the west, linked by the Mississippi to the markets of Europe and the world.[11] The Spanish decision to open the river to trade put an end to his plan.

Morgan had not confined himself to dreams while leaving practical formulations to others. His experiment in urban planning included an astonishing attention to detail that extended even to the naming of the streets. The eastern edge of the town lay along the riverfront. Serving as its spine, King Street bisected New Madrid from east to west. To the north, moving away from King, streets were named First North, Second North, and so on, and those to the south began with First South, and continued. The street fronting the river was called First River, followed by Second River, Third River, and so on to the western boundary. Each

10. Savelle, *George Morgan*, pp. 216–17; Jacobs, *Tarnished Warrior*, pp. 78–96; Foley, *History of Missouri*, p. 37.
11. Savelle, *George Morgan*, p. 211.

city block contained six acres, subdivided into twelve lots of a half acre each; the lots were numbered from the river, east to west, on each side of the street. Forty lots were reserved for "such purposes as the citizens shall from time to time recommend," but some uses were designated in advance. The number one lots on either side of King Street were set aside for a market and the number thirteen lots for a Roman Catholic church and school. The number thirteen lots on either side of every fifth north street and every fifth south street were reserved for the churches and schools of "such religious denominations as shall settle" in the city. Twelve acres were set aside for the king. Outside the town four acres were reserved at "every intersection of public roads or highways, throughout the whole territory," one each for a school, a church, the poor, and the king, and no farmhouse was to be more than two and a half miles from such a site.[12]

In his grand design Morgan revealed eccentricities that show him to be totally out of step with his time: He liked trees, Indians, and wild animals. Twelve acres were set aside for parks, with the trees to be left standing; trees were preserved on the parkway running along the riverfront, and it was forbidden to cut down a tree anywhere in the city without permission of a magistrate. For the sake of wild animals, he barred professional hunters altogether and forbade other hunting except for what would actually be consumed by the hunter and his family. "This regulation," he wrote, "is intended for the preservation of those animals, and for the benefit of neighbouring Indians, whose dependence is on hunting principally—this settlement being

12. Morgan's "General Directions," dated April 1789, written at New Madrid, in Louis Houck, ed., *The Spanish Regime in Missouri*, vol. 1 (Chicago: R. R. Donnelly and Sons, 1909), pp. 301–6, quotes on 302, 303, 304.

wholly agricultural and commercial, no encouragement shall be given to white men hunters."[13]

Morgan had chosen an impressive site. Below the junction of the Ohio, the Mississippi wound and coiled like a snake as it moved on its course to the Gulf of Mexico, flanked most of the way by low-lying banks that it overran easily during the great spring freshets. But in southeastern Missouri, just north and to the west of the Ohio junction in what became Scott County, a low terrace ridge of sand and clay arose and ran on a line west of but generally parallel to the river. Its height was not uniform, and low depressions bisecting it were a standing invitation at flood time. It finally touched the river at New Madrid. At this point the mighty stream had bitten deep into the side of the ridge, carving out banks seemingly secure from the highest flood. The town nestled in the crook of a horseshoe bend twenty-five miles in length, commanding a view six miles up-river and ten miles downstream. This strategic location effectively blocked the exit of the Ohio into the Mississippi. The current there brought the channel, and therefore all river traffic, very close to the western bank; and the mouth of bayou St. John, which was adjacent to the townsite, created a natural harbor. Both before and after the advent of steam power, New Madrid for several years was the most important landing place for boats between the Ohio junction and New Orleans with the exception of Natchez.[14]

13. Ibid., p. 305.

14. C. F. Marbut, "The Evolution of the Northern Part of the Lowlands of Southeastern Missouri," *The University of Missouri Studies* 1:3 (July 1902):10, 16. Also, Louis Houck, *A History of Missouri,* vol. 2 (New York: Arno Press and *New York Times*, 1971), p. 103; Zadok Cramer, *The Navigator*, 8th ed. (Pittsburgh: Cramer, Spear and Eichbaum, 1814), reprinted in Ethel C. Leahy, *Who's Who on the Ohio River and Its Tributaries* (Cincinnati: E. C. Leahy Publishing Co., 1931), pp. 177–78; Sir Charles Lyell, *A Second Visit to the*

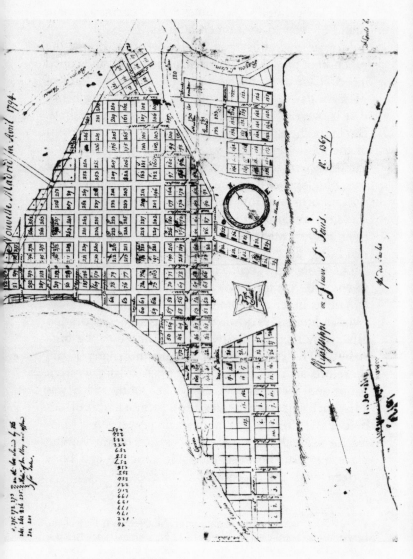

Plat of New Madrid, 1794
Provided by the Missouri Historical Society, St. Louis, Mo.

The town survived Morgan's departure. The Spanish built a fort and levied duties on river traffic, to the disgust of American boatmen. All that survived of the grand design was a rudimentary street plan. The earliest map to survive, dated 1794 (see p. 26), shows none of the parkways or green spaces. The street names were lost along the way, and the marketplace and school and church sites are nowhere evident. The fort and its grounds sit squarely in the middle on the river's front. The dream of a "great and magnificent city" had become, in reality, just another dreary frontier village.[15]

New Madrid had more than six hundred inhabitants in 1797, but most of the settlers who accompanied Morgan had long since returned to their homes. The site proved to be unhealthy—the surrounding countryside was poorly drained, and encouraged "putrid fevers and agues"—and the river "overflowed amazingly" during the first winter, apparently sweeping away the new government house.[16] Still, new settlers soon took their places, and the town acquired a decidedly French flavor. Many of the newcomers migrated from the Illinois country, attracted to the area by the liberal land policy of the Spanish. Indian refugees from the Ohio country also located nearby. One visitor re-

United States of North America, vol. 2 (New York: Harper and Brothers Publishers, 1849), pp. 173–74; Timothy Flint, *The History and Geography of the Mississippi Valley*, vol. 1 (Cincinnati: E. H. Flint and L. R. Lincoln, 1832), pp. 308–9.

15. John William Reps, "New Madrid on the Mississippi," Society of Architectural Historians *Journal* 18 (March 1959): 21–26; quote in Cramer, *The Navigator*, p. 177.

16. Houck, *Spanish Regime in Missouri*, vol. 2, p. 397; Foley, *History of Missouri*, p. 37; Savelle, *George Morgan*, p. 227; Thomas Ashe, *Travels in America* (London: Printed for Richard Phillips, 1809), p. 267; Georges Henri Victor Collot, *A Journey in North America*, vol. 2 (Paris: Printed for Arthus Bertrand, Bookseller, 1826), p. 18.

marked that the town's inhabitants included several "amiable and genteel families" with the "worthless and despicable part of society" well represented; a harsher judgment labeled them one and all the "dregs of Kentucky, France, and Spain." The district as a whole, including northeastern Arkansas, had a population of 1,350 whites and 150 slaves in 1804 when the territory came under the control of the United States, but the town had actually declined in size since 1797, perhaps by as much as a third.[17]

Morgan had decreed that at least one hundred feet should separate the eastern edge of his town from the river, but he had reckoned without the river.[18] The high commanding bank he had supposed to be the town's greatest asset proved to be its bane. This was noticed as early as 1796 (see p. 30):

> The river which by its direction strikes with force upon this perpendicular bank, carries away, at different periods of the year, a considerable quantity of the ground on which the town and fort are built; this ground being composed of earth, washed down by the waters, is easily dissolved. . . . Every annual revolution carries off from one to two hundred yards of this bank; so that the fort, built five years since at six hundred yards from the side of the river, has already lost all its covered way; and at the time we passed, the commander had given orders to empty the magazines and dislodge the artillery, having no doubt but that in the course of the winter the rest of the fort would be destroyed.[19]

17. Henry Marie Brackenridge, *Views of Louisiana: Together with a Journal of a Voyage up the Missouri River, in 1811* (Pittsburgh: Cramer, Spear and Eichbaum, 1814), pp. 129–30; Ashe, *Travels in America*, pp. 257–58; Samuel Prescott Hildreth, "History of a Voyage from Marietta to New Orleans in 1805," *The American Pioneer* 1 (1842):128; Edwin C. McReynolds, *Missouri: A History of the Crossroads State* (Norman: University of Oklahoma Press, 1962), p. 33; Foley, *History of Missouri*, p. 37; Savelle, *George Morgan*, p. 227.

18. Houck, *Spanish Regime in Missouri*, vol. 1, p. 304.

19. Collot, *Journey in North America*, vol. 2, pp. 17–18.

"Three forts, and a number of large and spacious streets have been taken away, within these fifteen years," wrote Henry Marie Brackenridge in 1811. A map dated 1810 (see p. 35) showed no sign of the old fortifications; two tiers of blocks were gone and the river had nibbled at a third.[20]

So irresistible was Morgan's grand design that men sometimes described New Madrid in glowing terms that seemed to contradict the general impressions of most travelers. But on the eve of the earthquakes the town rested on a wasting and doomed bank. According to Amos Stoddard, the army officer who accepted the transfer of Upper Louisiana in the name of the United States and served for a while as its interim governor, its original houses had been "erected over the present channel."[21] Its founder had hoped they would stand astride the wealth of a continent, but 1811 found the people of New Madrid locked in an endless, hopeless struggle with the unrelenting river that was to have been their highway to greatness.

What happened to this little village in the early morning hours of 16 December 1811 has been described many times. Most such descriptions relied heavily on two early published accounts. The first and more important was that of Eliza Bryan (sometimes spelled Bryant), which is authentic, but its author remains obscure. She clearly lived in New Madrid and experienced the earthquakes, but little else is known of her. In *Fury in the Earth: A Novel of the New Madrid Earth-*

---

20. Brackenridge, *Views of Louisiana,* pp. 129–30; Reps, "New Madrid on the Mississippi," p. 25; Francis Baily, *Journal of a Tour in Unsettled Parts of North America in 1796 and 1797* (London: Baily Brothers, 1856), p. 263; Ashe, *Travels in America,* pp. 267–68.

21. Hildreth, "History of a Voyage," p. 128; Amos Stoddard, *Sketches, Historical and Descriptive, of Louisiana* (Philadelphia: Mathew Carey, 1812), p. 209; Foley, *History of Missouri,* pp. 70–71.

Plan of the Fort at New Madrid, 1796
Georges Henri Victor Collot, *A Journey in North America, Atlas*
(Paris: Printed for Arthus Bertrand, Bookseller, 1826), pl. 30.
Courtesy of the Edward E. Ayer Collection, The Newberry Library,
Chicago, Ill.

quake, Harry Harrisson Kroll garnished her with a pro-
fession (schoolmarm) and a genealogy (descendant of
one of the witches burned at Salem Village), but while
this additional information cannot be refuted abso-
lutely, neither can it be confirmed.

Bryan's letter to the evangelist Lorenzo Dow was
included in his published journal.[22] She gave a brief
description of each of the major shocks, but her letter,
written in 1816, was a recollection of events already
four years old. Her memories of the first shock were
vivid: the awful noise; thunder that was loud but distant,
"hoarse and vibrating"; the cracking sound of falling
trees; the roaring of the river; a vapor; the smell of
sulphur; total darkness; and "the affrighted inhabitants
running to and fro." But the total effect of her narrative
was more cumulative than sequential. An accurate profile of each of the major series of shocks could not be
reconstructed; elements unique to them separately
were hard to distinguish.

The account most often cited was that included in
Timothy Flint's *Recollections of the Last Ten Years.* A
transplanted New Englander, Flint was a man of parts:
preacher, geographer, novelist, editor, booster, and
inveterate river rat. He visited New Madrid in 1819
and wrote a memorable narration based on interviews
with eyewitnesses. However, Flint made little effort to
establish sequence, and although many details are useful additions to the record, they were not much help in
distinguishing between the shocks. At times Flint could
be credulous. One much retold tale may have been the
result of his eagerness to establish the resourcefulness
of his hosts. During the hard shocks at nearby Little

22. Lorenzo Dow, *History of Cosmopolite; or, the Four Volumes of
Lorenzo Dow's Journal* (Wheeling, Va.: Joshua Martin, 1848), pp.
344–46.

31

Prairie, he wrote, fissures, sometimes "half a mile" in length, opened and threatened to swallow the people. "They felled the tallest trees at right angles to the chasms, and stationed themselves upon the felled trees. By this invention all were saved. For the chasms occurred more than once under these felled trees."[23] A mental picture of panic-stricken people rooting around in sheds for axes and coolly attacking dancing, weaving trees strains the imagination; but the idea of men, women, and children astride those trunks stretched across yawning chasms as the earth bucked and heaved like an angry mule falls, as resoundingly as they would have, of its own weight.

A contemporary account of the events of 16 December exists, although its author is unknown. This "Extract from a letter to a gentleman in Lexington, from his friend at New Madrid," dated 16 December, with entries for the seventeenth and the twenty-fourth, was printed first in the *Lexington Reporter* and later in the *Pennsylvania Gazette.* Samuel Latham Mitchill, a former occupant of the chair of natural history at Columbia College who had represented New York in both the U.S. House and Senate, compiled from newspaper accounts a detailed history of the effects of the earthquake around the country. He neglected, however, to cite his sources. He made use of the "New Madrid Extract" in a very reduced and somewhat inaccurate form.[24] In any event, condensation would mar the vividness of this document.

About 2 o'clock this morning we were awakened by a most tremendous noise, while the house danced about and seemed

23. Timothy Flint, *Recollections of the Last Ten Years* (New York: Alfred A. Knopf, 1932), p. 219.
24. Samuel Latham Mitchill, "A Detailed Narrative of the Earthquakes," *Transactions of the Literary and Philosophical Society of New York* 1 (1814):285.

as if it would fall on our heads. I soon conjectured the cause of our troubles, and cried out it was an Earthquake, and for the family to leave the house; which we found very difficult to do, owing to its rolling and jostling about. The shock was soon over, and no injury was sustained, except the loss of the chimney, and the exposure of my family to the cold of the night. At the time of this shock, the heavens were very clear and serene, not a breath of air stirring; but in five minutes it became very dark, and a vapour which seemed to impregnate the atmosphere, had a disagreeable smell, and produced a difficulty of respiration. I knew not how to account for this at the time, but when I saw, in the morning, the situation of my neighbours' houses, all of them more or less injured, I attributed it to the dust. . . . The darkness continued till daybreak; during this time we had EIGHT more shocks, none of them so violent as the first.

At half past 6 o'clock in the morning it cleared up, and believing the danger over I left home, to see what injury my neighbours had sustained. A few minutes after my departure there was another shock, extremely violent. I hurried home as fast as I could, but the agitation of the earth was so great that it was with much difficulty I kept my balance—*the motion of the earth was about twelve inches to and fro.* I cannot give you an accurate description of this moment; the earth seemed convulsed—the houses shook very much—chimnies [*sic*] falling in every direction. The loud, hoarse roaring which attended the earthquake, together with the cries, screams, and yells of the people, seems still ringing in my ears.

Fifteen minutes after seven o'clock, we had another shock. This one was the most severe one we have yet had—the darkness returned, and the noise was remarkably loud. The first motions of the earth were similar to the preceding shocks, but before they ceased we rebounded up and down, and it was with difficulty we kept our seats. At this instant I expected a dreadful catastrophe—the uproar among the people strengthened the colouring of the picture—the screams and yells were heard at a great distance. . . .

Tuesday, 17th—I never before thought the passion of fear so strong as I find it here among the people. It is really diverting, or would be so, to a disinterested observer, to see the rueful faces of the different persons that present themselves at my tent—some so agitated that they cannot speak—others cannot hold their tongues—some cannot sit still, but must be in constant motion, while others cannot walk. Several men, I am informed, on the night of the first shock deserted their families, and have not been heard of since. Encampments are formed of those that remain in the open fields, of 50 and 100 persons in each.[25]

The author of the "New Madrid Extract" added that "no white person" was lost as of 24 December, although six Indians in the vicinity had been killed. Years later, another visitor was shown "the sink-hole where the negro was drowned." Bryan said "a female" died of fright on 16 December. The death itself, and its cause, was not in question, but the date was. Godfrey Lesieur, a young boy at the time whose recollections as an adult have been quoted almost as much as Bryan's, gave the victim a name, Mrs. Lafont, and adds another, Mrs. Jarvis, who was fatally injured by a falling log. But Lesieur was not in New Madrid on 16 December, although his account certainly encompassed events there. He was a resident and son of the founder of Little Prairie and was probably among the one hundred refugees from that settlement who arrived in New Madrid on Christmas Eve. It was unlikely that in so small a community the author of the "New Madrid Extract" would have been ignorant of a death so dramatic—according to Flint the victim "ran as far as her strength would permit, and then fell exhausted and fainting, from which she never recovered"—nor would Lesieur have used the title "Mrs." without other attibution had the victim been Negro or Indian. The death probably occurred at a later time.[26]

25. Philadelphia *Pennsylvania Gazette*, 12 February 1812.

26. Lyell, *A Second Visit*, p. 176; Dow, *History of Cosmopolite*, p. 344; *History of Southeast Missouri* (Chicago: Goodspeed Publishing Co., 1888), p. 306, cited hereafter as *Goodspeed's History*; W. F. Switzler, *Switzler's Illustrated History of Missouri from 1541 to 1877*

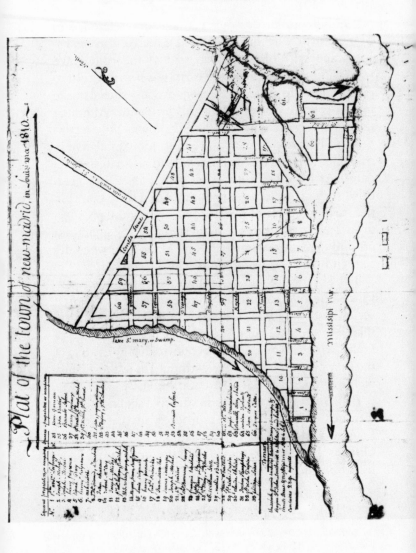

Plat of New Madrid, 1810
Provided by the Missouri Historical Society, St. Louis Mo.

Neither did the extract contain any reference to characteristic earthquake ground damage, such as fissures and sand blows. Bryan said of the cumulative effect of the shakes that "the earth was horribly torn to pieces," but she made no reference to any such damage in her specific discussion of the sixteenth. Although they certainly recounted such phenomena, the descriptions of Flint and Lesieur were both too cumulative in character to make it possible always to distinguish exact dates. As for other sources, as time passed exaggerations such as "streams of fire" emerging from cracks in the earth were apt to nestle down among the recollections. In fact, no evidence suggested that any significant ground damage occurred at New Madrid between the sixteenth and the twenty-fourth of December.[27]

The absence of damage supports the argument, advanced by one scholar, that the epicenter of the first series of shocks was farther away from New Madrid than was the case later.[28] Certainly the experience of Louis Bringier would seem to confirm that by the end of the first week in January the earthquakes in the vicinity of New Madrid had increased in intensity.

Bringier was a young scamp who had squandered the fortunes of himself and his brother, his partner in a Louisiana plantation, in the gambling dens of New Orleans. He fled in disgrace to live among the Indians, by whom he was adopted. (He may have become a

---

(St. Louis: C. R. Burns, 1879), p. 185; R. A. Campbell, ed., *Campbell's Gazetteer of Missouri* (St. Louis: R. A. Campbell, 1874), p. 395; Houck, *History of Missouri*, vol. 2, p. 159; Philadelphia *Pennsylvania Gazette*, 12 February 1812; Flint, *Recollections*, p. 217.

27. Dow, *History of Cosmopolite*, p. 345; F. C. Usher, "On the Elevation of the Banks of the Mississippi in 1811," *American Journal of Science and Arts* 31 (January 1837):295.

28. Otto W. Nuttli, "The Mississippi Valley Earthquakes of 1811 and 1812: Intensities, Ground Motion and Magnitudes," *Bulletin of the Seismological Society of America* 63:1 (19 February 1973):227–48.

chief, though in what tribe it is uncertain.) Later he returned to New Orleans to become a pillar of the community, at one time and another both city surveyor and surveyor-general of the state. In early January 1812, still in his primitive phase, he found himself in the neighborhood of New Madrid. He later wrote a paper for the *American Journal of Science and Arts* recounting his experience.[29]

The unique aspect of his description was the emphasis on ground damage. Great amounts of liquid spurted into the air.

It rushed out in all quarters, bringing with it . . . carbonized wood, reduced . . . to dust, which was ejected to the height of from ten to fifteen feet, and fell in a black shower, mixed with the sand which its rapid motion had forced along; at the same time, the roaring and whistling produced by the impetuosity of the air escaping from its confinement, seemed to increase the horrible disorder of the trees which everywhere encountered each other, being blown up, cracking and splitting, and falling by thousands at a time. In the meantime, the surface was sinking, and a black liquid was rising up to the belly of my horse, who stood motionless, struck with terror.

These occurrences occupied nearly two minutes; the trees . . . kept falling here and there, and the whole surface of the country remained covered with holes, which . . . resembled so many craters of volcanoes, surrounded with a ring of carbonized wood and sand, which rose to the height of about seven feet.[30]

Seven months later he measured these holes and found them to be no deeper than twenty feet, but by

29. Houck, *History of Missouri*, vol. 3, pp. 175–76; Louis Bringier, "Notices of the Geology, Mineralogy, Topography, Production, and Aboriginal Inhabitants of the Regions around the Mississippi and Its Confluent Waters," *American Journal of Science and Arts* 3 (1821):15–46.

30. Bringier, "Notices of the Geology," pp. 20–21. Bringier gave 6 January for the event but he probably confused the date. A shock such as he described occurred on 7 January.

that time a great deal of sand had washed into them. His description was the first with any reasonably established time sequence to give any indication of the changes wrought on the ground. The country, he said, was formerly comprised of small prairies or meadows interspersed among the woods. Afterwards it was covered with "slaches" (ponds) and sand hills.

The devastation of Little Prairie also indicated that the epicenter was farther away from New Madrid when the shocks commenced than was the case later. An educated guess for the location of the epicenter on 16 December placed it at the southern end of the lake formed by the St. Francis River in northeastern Arkansas.[31] This point was about sixty-five miles from New Madrid on a bias southwest by northeast. Thirty-two miles downstream, the tiny village of Little Prairie was only about forty miles from the epicenter on a similar bias. The difference in damage at this distance from the epicenter was considerable.

On Christmas Eve, nearly one hundred persons, virtually the entire population of Little Prairie, stumbled into New Madrid, led by an American miller named George Roddell (or Ruddell). The townspeople, mostly French—New Madrid was two-thirds American by 1811—had fled hastily from a scene of almost total destruction. Not a "single person was left but an old negro man probably too infirm to fly." They made their way north, according to one account, because they heard "the upper country was not damaged"; they walked the thirty-mile distance in three days.[32] The

31. Nuttli, "The Mississippi Valley Earthquakes," p. 231. "There is no way of precisely determining the epicenter of any of the 1811 and 1812 earthquakes." Nuttli to the author, 17 January 1975.

32. Philadelphia *Pennsylvania Gazette,* 12 February 1812; *New York Evening Post,* 11 February 1812; account of James Fletcher, *Pittsburgh Gazette*, 14 February 1812. A discrepancy in chronology

events that propelled them on their panic-stricken flight were described by Roddell to the author of the "New Madrid Extract."

He informs me that no material injury was sustained from the first shocks—when the 10th shock occurred, he was standing in his own yard, situated on the bank of the bayou of the Big Lake; the bank gave way, and sunk down about 30 yards from the water's edge, as far as he could see up and down the stream. It upset his mill, and one end of his dwelling house sunk down considerably; the surface on the opposite side of the Bayou, which before was swamp, became dry land; the side he was on became lower. His family at this time were running away from the house towards the woods; a large crack in the ground prevented their retreat into the open field. They had just assembled together when the eleventh shock came on, after which there was not perhaps a square acre of ground unbroken in the neighborhood, and in about fifteen minutes after the shock the water rose round them waist deep. The old gentleman in leading his family, endeavoring to find higher land, would sometimes be precipitated headlong into one of those cracks in the earth, which were concealed from the eyes by the muddy water through which they were wading. As they proceeded, the earth continued to burst open, and mud, water, sand and stone coal, were thrown up the distance of 30 yards—frequently trees of a large size were split open, fifteen or twenty feet up. After wading eight miles, he came to dry land.[33]

James Fletcher, who took part in the exodus to New Madrid, confirmed most of these details. In the early daylight hours the first really damaging shock occurred; about fifteen minutes later the entire townsite was flooded. Water spouted to great heights, as if it were

---

exists between this account and the "New Madrid Extract." The latter said the refugees arrived in New Madrid on 24 December, but Fletcher said they remained encamped on the place of François Lesieur (father of Godfrey) for eight days before departing, which means they would have left Little Prairie on 24 December. Possibly two distinct groups made the journey at different times.

33. Philadelphia *Pennsylvania Gazette,* 12 February 1812.

pressed "out of the pores of the earth." He believed that the whole country was sinking and fled in horror from the river. "The agitation of the earth was so great that it was with difficulty any could stand on their feet, and some could not."[34]

The merchant James McBride, with two heavily laden flatboats, tied up at the site in March. He quickly found that he was moored over part of the town, "now the bed of the Mississippi river." From the face of an adjacent bank coffins projected, remnants of a burial ground carried off by the water.[35] Three Frenchmen sheltered nearby in a rickety, makeshift shack that was thrown together with boards taken from collapsed houses. He walked over the area in the drizzling rain. Not a house remained standing:

> The surface of the ground was cracked in almost every direction. . . . But what particularly attracted my attention were circular holes in the earth from five or six to thirty feet in diameter, the depth corresponding with the diameter so as to be about half as deep as wide, and surrounded with a circle of sand two or three feet deep, and a black substance like stone coal.

The day was dark and gloomy; a constant noise rumbled ominously from deep within the earth. "All nature appeared in ruins, and seemed to mourn in solitude over her melancholy fate." He returned hastily to his boat, overcome by a "sudden dread."[36]

There is no adequate description of the effects of the shock of 23 January at New Madrid. Bryan wrote only

34. *Pittsburgh Gazette*, 14 February 1812.

35. Flint claimed the graveyard at New Madrid was carried off, also; Flint, *Recollections*, p. 215.

36. James McBride, "Brief Accounts of Journies in the Western Country, 1809–1812," *Quarterly Publication of the Historical and Philosophical Society of Ohio* 5:1 (January–March 1910):29–30. The little settlement of Point Pleasant, six miles below New Madrid, was also destroyed, but no chronology can be established for it.

that "one occurred as violent as the severest of the former ones." Between that time and 4 February "the earth was in continual agitation, visibly waving as a gentle sea." Beginning on the fourth the shocks began to increase in force. At three in the morning of the seventh the straining earth found release in a great convulsion, called by Bryan and others the "hard" shock.[37]

Accounts of the hard shock emphasized details not found earlier. Destruction of buildings, evacuation of people, and gravity of damage to the terrain were suddenly prominent. The epicenter of the earthquake was now very close to the town, and descriptions of the upheaval moved rapidly to a violent conclusion.

With good reason, after the shocks began, the people of New Madrid no longer trusted the shelter of their homes. According to the author of the "New Madrid Extract," they moved to tent encampments as early as 16 December. Later they built light wooden structures more adapted to their fears. The houses had remained standing, however; the earlier accounts all speak of chimneys toppling and other like damage but not of structures collapsing. This situation changed dramatically on 7 February. One boatman, seeking a safe haven on that day, said "the houses are all thrown down." Another witness said that there "was scarcely a house left entire—some wholly prostrated, others unroofed and not a chimney standing." Still another simply said "destroyed."[38]

All of the narratives agreed that the people fled the

37. Dow, *History of Cosmopolite*, p. 344.

38. Ibid., p. 345; Flint, *Recollections*, p. 219; Philadelphia *Pennsylvania Gazette*, 18 March 1812; Vincent Nolte, *Fifty Years in Both Hemispheres; or, Reminiscences of a Merchant's Life* (London: Trubner and Co., 1854), p. 182.

townsite entirely. Lesieur said the flight began 7 January during the shock described so vividly by Bringier. However, there was no question that something on the scale of a mass evacuation took place on 7 February. Furthermore, it took place precipitantly, in the dark, probably immediately following the hard shock. Boatmen viewing the town in the early morning daylight hours found "the inhabitants moved off, except the French, who live in camps close to the river side."[39]

It is not difficult to imagine the panic that prevailed. They "fled in terror from their falling dwellings," said a man who took part in the exodus.[40] Many had the presence of mind to hitch teams and load family and provisions. But in at least one case, family affection was no match for blind fear:

A young woman about seventeen years of age, named Betsy Masters, had been left by her parents and family, her leg having been broken below the knee by the falling of one of the weight-poles of the roof of the cabin; and, though a total stranger, I was the only person who would consent to return and see whether she still survived. Receiving a description of the locality of the place, I started, and found the poor girl upon a bed, as she had been left, with some water and corn bread within her reach. I cooked up some food for her, and made her condition as comfortable as circumstances would allow and returned the same day to the grand encampment.[41]

The few Frenchmen who elected to remain in the town kept an assortment of skiffs and canoes very close at hand in the event "the earth should sink." These boats became precious, indeed. One woman, marooned in the town when the flatboat on which she was traveling

39. Report from Russelville, Ky., in Philadelphia *Pennsylvania Gazette,* 18 March 1812, and account by Mathias Speed; and Nolte, *Fifty Years in Both Hemispheres,* p. 182.

40. John Shaw, "New Madrid Earthquake: Account of Colonel John Shaw," *Missouri Historical Review* 6 (January 1912):91.

41. Ibid., pp. 91–92.

was swamped, "offered a likely negro fellow for the use of a boat for a few hours," in order to retrieve her possessions, "but could not get it."[42]

Finally, there is no evidence with a date attached to it of significant ground damage in the town before the hard shock—Bringier claimed to be in the "vicinity," but nowhere indicated he had entered the town itself. The first such evidence appears in the record of 7 February. Speaking of sand blows, Bringier's "volcano" craters, Mathias Speed, a boatman who reached the town on the seventh and remained five days, said: "In the town of New Madrid there were four, but neither [sic] of them had vented stone or sand—the size of them, in diameter, varied from 12 to 50 feet, and in depth from 5 to 10 feet from the surface to the water."[43]

The obstacles encountered by those who fled the stricken town in the early morning hours indicate a greater magnitude of destructiveness than that described earlier by Bringier but similar to the havoc already experienced at Little Prairie. The wilderness surrounding New Madrid was diverse. Besides the meadows interspersed through forests mentioned by Bringier, the region also embraced cypress swamps, a bayou, lakes, and ponds. In some instances the bottoms of streams, lakes, and ponds were actually thrust up, their waters running off to flood the surrounding land to a depth of one to three feet. The water was tepid, "over blood heat," despite the chill temperature.[44]

42. Philadelphia *Pennsylvania Gazette*, 18 March 1812.
43. Ibid.
44. Shaw, "New Madrid Earthquake," p. 92; Timothy Dudley, "The Earthquake of 1811 at New Madrid, Missouri (from the Narrative of an Eyewitness)," *Annual Report of the Board of Regents of the Smithsonian Institution . . . for the Year 1858* (Washington: William A. Harris, Printer, 1859), p. 422. Testimony concerning the warm temperature of the water, especially extruded water, despite the wintry chill, was not uncommon. For instance, a man standing

While some areas were uplifted, much of the timber-land around the town had sunk as much as six feet. Fissures slashed and scarred the route, seriously inhibiting flight. Sand blows, the result of frightening eruptions of sand, coal, and other organic matter, dotted the landscape.[45]

An ominous development was the settling of the townsite. Zadok Cramer, author of *The Navigator,* a celebrated river guide, said he passed the town in the spring of 1811

before the earthquake, and in the winter of 1812, after it, and it appeared evident that it had sunk several feet; this appears further confirmed by the bank of the river about a mile below the town being considerably higher than the town, and looks like a natural second bank, of considerable elevation above the first.[46]

Bradbury was the first to mention this, indirectly. Repeating a rumor that reached him on Christmas Eve, he described the town as inundated, "become a lake," which given its considerable height implied a settling had taken place. This was inaccurate, however. The town was not flooded on 16 December, and although water appears to have washed over a part of the town during the course of the hard shocks on 7 February, by morning it had receded. No observer of that day spoke of flood waters. Whether or not it began to some degree

---

next to one of those explosions that created sand blows watched the hole fill immediately with water. He thrust in his arm and "found it warm." Philadelphia *Pennsylvania Gazette*, 18 March 1812. Lesieur, at Little Prairie on 16 December, said the water thrown up by eruptions "was lukewarm, so warm, indeed, as to produce no chilly sensation while swimming and wading through it." Campbell, *Gazetteer of Missouri*, p. 396.

45. Shaw, "New Madrid Earthquake," p. 92; Philadelphia *Pennsylvania Gazette*, 18 March 1812. One wonders if the author of the "New Madrid Extract" still found the scene "diverting."

46. Cramer, *The Navigator*, p. 178.

New Madrid

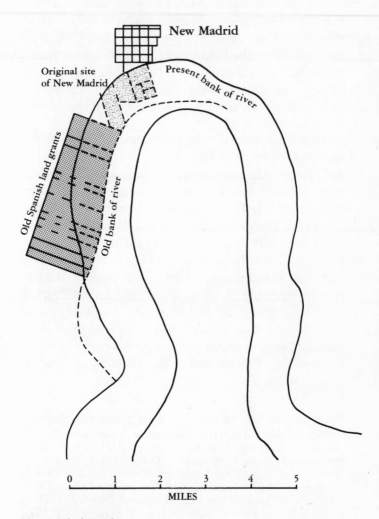

New Madrid Bend
The channel ca. 1912 and the river's course before 1811. Myron L. Fuller, "The New Madrid Earthquake," U.S. Geological Survey *Bulletin* 494 (Washington: Government Printing Office, 1912): 93, fig. 17. Provided by The John Crerar Library, Chicago, Ill.

earlier, the only dated testimony for the sinking is for 7 February. For instance, Mathias Speed said the former elevation of the bank was twenty-five feet. When he first saw it after the hard shock, "about breakfast time," it was twelve or thirteen feet. Bryan said the site sank fifteen feet. This settling continued until the spring floods, when the town was swallowed entirely by the river.[47]

About the time the river consumed New Madrid, making good on a threat as old as the town, on 26 March 1812, the Venezuelan cities of Caracas and La Guaira were thrown down. Twenty thousand people were killed that Holy Thursday, many of them buried alive in churches. The government of the United States appropriated fifty thousand dollars for the relief of the stricken region. In January 1814 it was urged to show the same consideration for its own citizens by the territorial assembly of Missouri. A year later Congress responded with an act, introduced by Missouri's territorial delegate, Col. Rufus Easton, allowing those with damaged land to exchange it for property elsewhere in the territory.[48] According to the historian of Missouri Louis Houck:

47. Reuben Gold Thwaites, ed., *Early Western Travels, 1748–1846*, vol. 5: *Bradbury's Travels in the Interior of America, 1809–1811* (Cleveland: Arthur H. Clark Co., 1904), pp. 210–11; Philadelphia *Pennsylvania Gazette*, 18 March 1812; Dow, *History of Cosmopolite*, p. 345; Myron L. Fuller, "The New Madrid Earthquake," U.S. Geological Survey *Bulletin* 494 (Washington: Government Printing Office, 1912):68–69; James T. Lloyd, *Lloyd's Steamboat Directory and Disasters on the Western Waters* (Cincinnati: J. T. Lloyd Co., 1856), p. 321.

48. E. Taylor Parks, "Foreign Aid—150 Years Ago," *Foreign Service Journal* 39:7 (July 1962):36–39. Clarence Edwin Carter, ed., *Territorial Papers of the United States*, vol. 14: *Louisiana–Missouri, 1806–1814* (Washington: Government Printing Office, 1949), pp. 729–30. Richard Peters, ed., *Public Statutes at Large of the United States of America*, vol. 3 (Boston: Charles C. Little and James Brown, 1846), pp. 211–12.

The actual sufferers were in nearly every instance defrauded. Before they had knowledge of the passage of the Act . . . the . . . county was filled with speculators from St. Louis who purchased their property at a rate of from forty to sixty dollars per claim, a claim sometimes embracing as much as six hundred and forty acres of land. After so acquiring the rights to the injured land, certificates of dislocation were issued by the St. Louis land-office to the purchasers of these injured properties. The owners of these certificates . . . hunted around for the most valuable public property and located their certificates on it. The demand for certificates being very great the more unscrupulous and dishonest New Madrid settlers would sell their claims several times to new speculators anxious to buy. All this led to endless litigation. . . . Much valuable property was located in North Missouri in the Boonslick country, and near the city of St. Louis, and also near Chicago. One François Langlois attempted to secure the Hot Springs of Arkansas with a New Madrid certificate.[49]

For the most part, claims were paid for in Missouri bank notes, which depreciated into worthlessness even more rapidly than the banks themselves failed, increasing the dimensions of the swindle. Congress passed three more acts over the next thirty years in futile attempts at clarification. Ten separate opinions by United States attorneys general slashed weakly at the knot. In 1845 the Supreme Court was still trying to unravel the tangled skeins. The harm was never undone. By 1820 "New Madrid claim" was as much a synonym for fraud as "continental dollar" had once been for worthlessness.[50]

49. Houck, *History of Missouri*, vol. 3, 179–80; Walter Lowrie, ed., *American State Papers: Documents Legislative and Executive of the Congress of the United States in Relation to Public Lands from the First Session of the First Congress to the First Session of the Twenty-third Congress: March 4, 1789 to June 15, 1834* (Washington: Duff-Green, 1834), vol. 3, pp. 437–39; vol. 4, pp. 39–47, 155, 749, 806, 811–14, 872, 881–85; vol. 6, pp. 184–85, 342–43, 409.

50. Daughters of the American Revolution, Lucy Jefferson Lewis

The New Madrid Earthquakes

Meanwhile, the stricken region fared poorly. In 1810, after six years of American rule, the population of what later became New Madrid County was 3,165. The impact of the earthquakes can be seen in the precipitant decline from that figure. In 1820 the county had a population of 2,296; ten years later it had increased by only 54 persons.[51]

The single most important reason for this decline was probably the continuation of the earthquakes. Although they were sharply reduced in intensity after the spring of 1812, tremors continued to be felt for many years thereafter.[52] For those who remained the earthquakes gradually became quotidian, and of little moment.

Several ladies and gentlemen, passengers on board a steam boat ascending the Mississippi in 1820, went on shore near New Madrid. In one of the houses, which they entered, they found a small collection of books. As they were amusing themselves with the examination of these, they felt the whole house so violently shaken, that they were scarcely able to stand upon their feet. Some consternation was, of course,

Chapter (New Madrid), "New Madrid Earthquakes, 1811–12, compiled from the New Madrid archive in New Madrid county courthouse," manuscript in Missouri Historical Society Library, St. Louis, Mo.; Peters, *Public Statutes at Large*, vol. 3, p. 417; vol. 4, pp. 482–83; vol. 5, p. 603; A. J. Bentley, ed., *Digest of the Official Opinions of the Attorneys General of the United States Comprising All of the Published Opinions Contained in Volumes I through XV Inclusive, and Embracing the Period from 1789 to 1881* (Washington: Government Printing Office, 1885), p. 376; Barry V. Gamble, 1845, in Benjamin C. Howard, ed., *Reports of Cases Argued and Adjudged in the Supreme Court of the United States, January Term, 1845*, vol. 3 (Philadelphia: T. and J. W. Johnson, 1845), pp. 32–57. Also *The Century Edition of the American Digest: A Complete Digest of All Reported American Cases, 1658–1896*, vol. 41 (St. Paul: West Publishing Co., 1903), pp. 143–49.

51. Campbell, *Gazetteer of Missouri*, p. 393.

52. Flint, *Recollections*, p. 222; Thomas Nuttall, *A Journal of Travels into the Arkansa Territory*, vol. 63 (Ann Arbor: University Microfilms, 1966), p. 46.

felt, and much terror expressed. "Don't be alarmed," said the lady of the house, "it is nothing but an earthquake."[53]

For prospective settlers, however, the almost daily occurrence of tremors was ample reason for avoiding the area. During the 1830s the population once again climbed to the level it had reached in 1810, and by 1840 was 4,554.[54] This rise coincided with a significant decrease in the frequency of the shakes.

The pattern of growth for the town of New Madrid was less directly attributable to the earthquakes. Obviously, it was an already wasting bank that sank, and the town—or parts of it—had already "sunk" several times when the earthquakes occurred. Long accustomed to retreating as street after street was carried away by the annual flood waters, the citizens of the town rebuilt again when the earthquakes subsided.

In 1806 one traveler complained bitterly that he could not get "a loaf of bread in the town, nor any kind of provisions whatever, though I offered any price." Two days before the shocks began, Bradbury found a "few straggling houses, situated round a plain of from two to three hundred acres . . . only two stores . . . indifferently furnished." Rebuilt, it looked much the same. Even though many families had moved away, a year after the disaster began there were still "two badly supplied stores," a tavern, and a post office. It remained the seat of a territorial district court, although Congress soon found it necessary to make other provisions for northeastern Arkansas because the roads to New Madrid had become impassable.[55]

The quakes, of course, hastened the process of decay.

53. Edwin James, *Account of an Expedition from Pittsburgh to the Rocky Mountains*, vol. 65 (Ann Arbor: University Microfilms, 1966), pp. 325–26.
54. Campbell, *Gazetteer of Missouri*, p. 393.
55. Ashe, *Travels in America*, pp. 267–68; *Bradbury's Travels*, p.

The botanist Thomas Nuttall, a visitor in 1818, found an "insignificant" hamlet, "containing little more than about 20 log houses," and the usual stores "miserably supplied." The houses before the earthquakes had been somewhat more pleasing to the eye. Reflecting the French influence, many were "painted white, with wide verandas or piazzas."[56] According to Flint, in 1819 the area "had the most melancholy of all aspects of decay, the tokens of former cultivation and habitancy, which were now mementos of desolation and desertion. Large and beautiful orchards, left uninclosed, houses uninhabited, deep chasms in the earth, obvious at frequent intervals—such was the face of the country."[57]

Morgan's vision of greatness died slowly, perhaps because Cramer described it in detail in *The Navigator,* and the town continued to enjoy a reputation sharply at variance with reality. Almost all travelers were curious to see what had come of this elaborate scheme. They were, without exception, disappointed. "This place has been finely described," said one, "and appears to better advantage on paper, then when under a *coup d'oeil.*" Another thought the "celebrity" of New Madrid "must astonish those who ever visited the place in open day." The annual encroachment of the river on the bank continued, and the town long remained, as one poetic traveler put it, not a town at all "but a vast, open terrain, on which the houses seem to flee from one another."[58]

201; Cramer, *The Navigator,* p. 177; Fuller, "New Madrid Earthquake," p. 21; Mitchill, "Detailed Narrative," pp. 304–5.

56. Nuttall, *Journal of Travels into Arkansa*, p. 46; Hildreth, "History of a Voyage," p. 128.

57. Flint, *Recollections*, p. 220.

58. Samuel R. Brown, *The Western Gazetteer; or, Emigrants Directory* (Auburn, N.Y.: H. C. Southwick, 1817), p. 206; William Darby, *The Emigrant's Guide to the Western and Southwestern States and Territories* (New York: Kirk and Merclin, 1818), p. 141; Reps, "New Madrid on the Mississippi," p. 26.

New Madrid

Sir Charles Lyell, British author of *Principles of Geology,* paid a second visit to the United States in 1845. As founder of the uniformitarian school, which minimized the role of catastrophes in forming the earth's crust, he had a natural interest in the earthquakes. Having talked in New Orleans with Bringier, by this time well into his respectable period, he decided to visit the site himself and arrived there in March 1846. He spent several days in New Madrid, making a cursory examination of the surrounding countryside. Like other commentators who observed the scene after the earthquakes, he was inclined to blame them for the generally primitive and decayed condition of the town (he and his wife were forced to lodge with a baker in a room scarcely large enough to hold a bed because the town had no inn). But Lyell recognized another limitation to the town's growth. He peered over the bank at three houses "fallen in during the last week," and predicted: "The steamboats, which are now sailing close to the bank, will, in a few years, pass freely over the site of the humble mansion where we had been sleeping; and the geographer, in constructing a map half a century hence, may have to transfer to the State of Kentucky, the spot where I saw a garden flourish."[59]

This prediction came true.

59. Lyell, *A Second Visit*, pp. 172–82, quote on pp. 173–74. Today the town is situated behind a levee and cannot be seen from the river.

3. The Mississippi River

A man who was on the river in a boat at the time of one of the shocks, declares he saw the mighty Mississippi *cut in twain*, while the waters poured down a vast chasm into the bowels of the earth.

James T. Lloyd, *Lloyd's Steamboat Directory and Disasters on the Western Waters* (1856)

    The effect of the shakes was most dramatic upon the river. There was heavy traffic upon the Mississippi in mid-December. Overland travel to the east coast was far more arduous and costly than water transport, and the river had become the principal highway of commerce for the settlements west of the Appalachian barrier. As a highway it had a severe limitation, however; until the era of steam, movement upriver against the current depended on muscle power. That era dawned in the year of the earthquakes. The first steamboat to navigate western waters left the vicinity of Louisville, en route to Natchez, as the shocks commenced. The number of boats upon the river made it the scene of many casualties, far more than on land, although no precise figure can be determined. It was also the setting for spectacular natural phenomena that were as terrifying as anything that occurred on the ground.

    As in the case of New Madrid, the events of 23 January were largely absent from the record. Frigid January temperatures and ice on the Ohio deterred the most hardy venturers; boatmen were a principal source for the details of earthquake damage, both on the river and for localities along it. By early February traffic had begun to trickle down the waterway again, and satisfying descriptions of the seventh exist.

Cumulative descriptions, which were designed mainly to assess the harmful effects on the flow of commerce, were useful as a measure of the full impact of the shakes on the river's course. In a letter to Cramer dated 18 February that was intended to help revise *The Navigator*, James Smith described in detail "the wonderful changes for the worse" inflicted on the river. He "found little from the mouth of Ohio to New Madrid, from which place to the Chickasaw Bluffs, or Fort Pickering [the site of Memphis], the face of the river is wholly changed."[1] His account was concerned primarily with the stretch between the second and fourth Chickasaw Bluffs above the site of Memphis. In this area the numerous islands and badly clogged channels had become a serious hazard to navigation. Smith's account contained no details of damage around New Madrid. Another narrative, which appeared anonymously in the *Bardstown* (Kentucky) *Repository*, spoke of "very dangerous falls . . . both above and below New Madrid."[2] Smith's failure to mention so noticeable a feature indicated that it had disappeared by the time he passed the site. But the falls of the Bardstown account were formed on 7 February, when the epicenter had moved northward to a location nearer New Madrid; the severe damage in the vicinity of the Chickasaw Bluffs was due east of the 16 December epicenter.

1. *Pittsburgh Gazette,* 13 March 1812.

2. Letter from "A Citizen of Kentucky," *Bardstown Repository* (n.d.), in National Archives, Record Group 59, Department of State, vol. 1, "Territorial Papers, Minnesota–Missouri," p. 32. Hereafter cited as "Bardstown Letter."

"Scene of the Great Earthquake in the West"
Our First Century: One Hundred Great and Memorable Events (1877), p. 220, in The State Historical Society of Missouri, Columbia, Mo.

The New Madrid Earthquakes

Rivercraft, whether the slender keelboats or the clumsy box-shaped flatboats, generally moored for the night at islands or at convenient points along the bank of the river, which was far too hazardous to navigate in the dark.[3] For protection they often moved in small fleets. On the evening of 15 December clusters of vessels dotted the river at intervals between New Madrid and Natchez, most of their crews asleep. With remarkable unity for witnesses so widely scattered, boatmen testified to the suddenness of the onset of quakes in the early morning hours. They were awakened by a "terrible shock and jarring of the boats"; followed by a "noise similar to that which would have been produced by running over a sand bar" or "grounding on gravel."[4] Some men grabbed weapons and prepared to repel an Indian attack. There was much shouting back and forth between boats in an effort to determine the cause of the sudden jolt. Those with cooler heads ran to the mooring lines to see if the boats were still secure, or took a sounding to see if they were aground, but most were overcome by panic in the black night as the mounting roar of the earthquake enveloped them. Those who remained moored to islands on the river through the successive shocks until daylight were relatively safe. Boats tied up alongside vertical banks on the western shore were in great peril, however, for if the banks collapsed they were crushed or swamped.

3. "In flat-boat journeys like ours it is a rule never to trust your craft in the night to the force of the current." Vincent Nolte, *Fifty Years in Both Hemispheres; or, Reminiscences of a Merchant's Life* (London: Trubner and Co., 1854), p. 181.

4. James H. Perkins, *Annals of the West* (Cincinnati: J. R. Albach, 1846), p. 520; Samuel Prescott Hildreth, "History of a Voyage from Marietta to New Orleans in 1805," *The American Pioneer 1* (1842): 129–30; *New York Evening Post,* 11 February 1812; New Orleans *Louisiana Gazette and Daily Advertiser,* 20 January 1812; *Pittsburgh Gazette,* 31 January 1812.

The Mississippi River

Virtually everyone got underway with first light, some not a moment too soon. "It was indeed providential that we had started," wrote one boatman. "The bank to which we were (but a few moments since) attached, was rent and fell into the river, whilst the trees rushed from the forests, precipitating themselves into the water with a force sufficient to have dashed us into a thousand atoms."[5]

Much of the sound and commotion in the dark was caused by the falling banks, although this fact was not always revealed until daylight. The shocks continued sporadically as the boats moved downstream that day. Boatmen from Little Prairie to the mouth of the St. Francis watched in awe as the banks along their route collapsed. They fell in "large columns"; in some places "five, ten and fifteen acres . . . sunk down in a body"; "on our right," said another, "there fell at once about 30 or 40 acres of land—some say 300 acres." Obviously, these figures are open to question; they vary not only with the location but with the excitability of individual observers. Yet Zadok Cramer, a careful man, confirmed the general impression. "In many places," he wrote, "the banks of the river . . . sunk hundreds of acres together, leaving the tops of the trees to be seen above the water." William Leigh Pierce saw a tree torn from the bank and "hurled with tremendous force into the river . . . where it . . . planted into the bed . . . there to stand, a terror to future navigators."[6]

While seldom high, the falling banks would

5. *New York Evening Post,* 11 February 1812.

6. Perkins, *Annals of the West,* p. 520; New Orleans *Louisiana Gazette and Daily Advertiser,* 20 January 1812; *Pittsburgh Gazette,* 31 January 1812, and 21 February 1812; Zadok Cramer, *The Navigator* 8th ed. (Pittsburgh: Cramer, Spear and Eichbaum, 1814), reprinted in Ethel C. Leahy, *Who's Who on the Ohio River and Its Tributaries* (Cincinnati: E. C. Leahy Publishing Co., 1931), p. 179; *New York Evening Post,* 11 February 1812.

The New Madrid Earthquakes

"Steamer Naviguant sur le Missouri"
"Voyage Dans Les Mauvaises Terres Du Nebraska," M. E. De Girardiu, *Le Tour Du Monde* (1849–1850), in The State Historical Society of Missouri, Columbia, Mo.

explain—if no other reasons existed—the ubiquitous agitation of the water's surface. The sudden impact of earth, trees, and other debris on so large a scale created enormous swells. This would explain, also, the persistent notion that the river ran backward during the first series of shocks. The swells produced tidal-wave effects in which "the waters of the Mississippi were seen to rise up like a wall in the middle of the stream, and then suddenly rolling back would beat against either bank with terrific force." Anyone who has been moored on the river when a modern towboat passed in the channel would have an inkling of the tremendous force exerted. Boats were swamped, their crews drowned and cargoes lost; others "were ... cast 'high and dry' upon the shores." The latter occurred at New Madrid, where richly laden boats were washed up the mouth of bayou St. John and left stranded by the receding waters. Whatever their problems, the citizens of the town were never short of supplies.[7]

There were a number of reports of a dramatic rise in the level of the river of between three and fourteen feet and of a plunge just as sudden. As the water rose the current was noticeably quickened. Most testimonials to this phenomenon were second hand, but one—a firsthand account printed in *The Navigator*—was unequivocal, although it said nothing about a sudden plunge: "the water rose after the first shock 7 or 8 feet perpendicular, and the current ran from 7 to 8 miles per hour."[8] Given the peculiarities of local conditions, any

---

7. Lorenzo Dow, *History of Cosmopolite; or, the Four Volumes of Lorenzo Dow's Journal* (Wheeling, Va.: Joshua Martin, 1848), pp. 344–46; James T. Lloyd, *Lloyd's Steamboat Directory and Disasters on the Western Waters* (Cincinnati: J. T. Lloyd and Co., 1856), p. 320; Perkins, *Annals of the West*, p. 520–21; Timothy Flint, *Recollections of the Last Ten Years* (New York: Alfred A. Knopf, 1932), p. 219.

8. Cramer, *The Navigator*, p. 179; Samuel Latham Mitchill, "A

or all of these observations could be accurate within a restricted area, but all three—a rise, a quickening, a sudden fall—were probably not general over the entire affected area. Pierce, whose detailed observations were based on notes made at the time, traversed almost the entire stretch affected during the first series of shocks. He noted the quickening of the current and compared this to the "times of the highest floods," when the water ran at a rate of four or five knots per hour.[9] Clocking his time over a distance of fifty-two miles, he concluded that the river was moving at a rate of six knots, a figure close to the seven or eight miles per hour given in *The Navigator* letter. However, Pierce said specifically that the water was low, and made no mention of a sudden rise. He did say that the river fell still further with "astonishing rapidity." The problem is to distinguish between fact and legend. The notion of a quick rise followed by an even more sudden fall of the water's level was the origin of the popular belief that the river was "cut in twain," that it poured down "some great opening in the earth." Pierce toyed with this idea when the river suddenly fell but discarded it when the evidence failed to materialize as he proceeded downstream, and nothing he heard from other boatmen led him to revive it.[10]

The earthquake legends, like most folklore, generally have a basis in fact, and the belief that the river poured into subterranean chambers is no exception.

Detailed Narrative of the Earthquakes," *Transactions of the Literary and Philosophical Society of New York* 1 (1814):293; John Haywood, *The Natural and Aboriginal History of Tennessee* (Nashville: George Wilson, 1823), p. 30; New Orleans *Louisiana Gazette and Daily Advertiser*, 14 January 1812 and 20 January 1812.

9. It may be that the association between floods and fast water created in some people an illusion of the river's rise.

10. Haywood, *The Natural and Aboriginal History of Tennessee*, p. 32; *New York Evening Post*, 11 February 1812.

The bed of the river east of the 16 December epicenter did not escape the kind of disturbances common to dry land. Fissures must have opened and closed, contributing to the general turbulence of the water. Sand blows, eruptions that left behind deep circular craters on dry land, occurred in the river's bed. If they were deep enough they could have created a whirlpool effect, known indelicately as "sucks," powerful enough to pull a boat down with it. Sucks were sighted near New Madrid on 7 February. None were recorded for 16 December but might have occurred in isolated instances. Certainly there is evidence of sand blows. Pierce, in common with many boatmen, was puzzled by the sound of explosions resembling the discharge of artillery. In the dark he was unable to determine the cause, but it was readily apparent during the daylight shocks.

There was a volcanic discharge of combustible matter to a great height, as incessant rumbling was heard below, and the bed of the river was excessively agitated, whilst the water assumed a turbid and boiling appearance—near our boat a spout of confined air, breaking its way through the waters, burst forth, and with a loud report discharged mud, sticks, &c, from the river's bed, at least thirty feet above the surface. These spoutings were frequent, and in many places appeared to rise to the very Heavens. . . . One of the spouts [directly under our boat] would inevitably [have] sunk it, and, probably [would] have blown it into a thousand fragments.[11]

One can easily visualize the turbulence of the water as the banks collapsed and the bed erupted. Whole sections of forest fell with the banks and the surface of the river was covered with floating trees, which bunched in channel narrows such as the Devil's Race Ground, creating nearly impassable barriers. Many of these trees came from the river's bottom rather than the

11. *New York Evening Post,* 11 February 1812.

banks. They bobbed to the surface and joined a parade of debris at times "so thick that it appeared impossible for a boat to find a passage." Some commentators were skeptical of waterlogged trees flaunting the physical laws of nature. They seemed to eyewitnesses to be of a great age, dating even to antiquity: "hundreds of old trees that had lain perhaps half a century at the bottom of the river, appeared"; "large trees, which had lain for ages at the bottom . . . shot up"; "every tree . . . since Noah's flood . . . stands . . . out of the water."[12] Testimony was too profuse to doubt that a rising of the trees occurred, but their age was exaggerated. In the best of times the river was infested with planters and sawyers, against which floating trees lodged, eventually piling up in tiers; the weight of thick sediment carried by the river built up and pressed the lower levels against the bottom.[13] The river carried so much silt that trees dislodged only a few months earlier lay on the bottom, their buoyant properties still partly intact, until the disturbance of the earthquakes released their muddy bonds.

A number of islands were reported to have sunk during the first series, incontestable evidence of the power of the earthquakes. The islands of the Mississippi ranged in size from little more than bars with a few willows to expanses of heavily forested land several miles in extent, inundated only during the highest freshets. From the available evidence the destruction of these mighty tracts was limited to a stretch of the river south of the vicinity of the first Chickasaw Bluff.

12. Cramer, *The Navigator,* p. 179; New Orleans *Louisiana Gazette and Daily Advertiser,* 20 January 1812; *New York Evening Post,* 11 February 1812; *Pittsburgh Gazette,* 31 January 1812.

13. "Trees more capable of floating will be cloged [*sic*] in the accumulated mud in the bottom and lodged against the Trees projecting above the water, on the margin of the old Channel and thus it may be intirely Chocked [*sic*] up."—"Bardstown Letter."

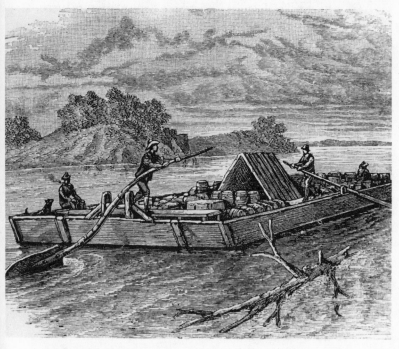

Flatboat on the Mississippi
Samuel A. Drake, *The Making of the Great West* (1891), p. 164, in
The State Historical Society of Missouri, Columbia, Mo.

Lorenzo Dow, the evangelist who printed Bryan's letter, said two islands near New Madrid were washed away; but Cramer, who numbered each island from the mouth of the Ohio, made no mention of this loss in *The Navigator*. There were various other accounts of islands sinking with no indication of their location or identity. The first island identified by Cramer as missing after the earthquakes was number thirty-two, formerly about three miles long and with a heavy growth of timber, located five miles above the first Chickasaw Bluff. He mentions only one other, number ninety-four.[14]

Eyewitness reports from south of the fourth Chickasaw Bluff are more scarce than was the case north to New Madrid, but it was clearly a zone of intense convulsion. Island number ninety-four was three hundred miles below the fourth Chickasaw Bluff. The cutoff point in severity was somewhere between the doomed island and Natchez, which, although shocks were felt there strongly, suffered only slight damage and some collapse of banks. Twenty miles below Natchez the shocks could scarcely be felt on the river. Four hundred miles to the north, near the mouth of the St. Francis, the settlement of Big Prairie ("formerly considerable" according to Cramer) was destroyed.[15] Midway between

14. Dow, *History of Cosmopolite*, p. 346; Cramer, *The Navigator*, pp. 180, 189; Timothy Dudley, "The Earthquake of 1811 at New Madrid, Missouri (from the Narrative of an Eyewitness)," *Annual Report of the Board of Regents of the Smithsonian Institution . . . for the Year 1858* (Washington: William A. Harris, Printer, 1859), p. 423.

15. Winthrop Sargent, "Account of Several Shocks of an Earthquake in the Southern and Western Parts of the United States," *Memoirs of the American Academy of Arts and Sciences* 3:2 (1815):351; New Orleans *Louisiana Gazette and Daily Advertiser,* 31 December 1811; Cramer, *The Navigator,* pp. 184–85; Thomas Nuttall, *A Journal of Travels into the Arkansa Territory,* vol. 63 (Ann Arbor: University Microfilms, 1966), p. 58. Distances here follow the line of the river as given in *The Navigator*. The distances in a straight line were much shorter.

there and Natchez was island number ninety-four. It had been small but apparently well known as a haven of river pirates; its name was Stack or Crow's Nest Island, but Cramer hinted that Rogue's Nest would have been more appropriate. That conclusion seemed justified by the only surviving account of the island's disappearance, in which the adventures of a Captain Sarpy of St. Louis were related.

They tied up at this island on the evening of the 15th of December, 1811. In looking around they found that a party of river pirates occupied part of the island and were expecting Sarpy with the intention of robbing him. As soon as Sarpy found that out he quietly dropped lower down the river. In the night the earthquake came and next morning when the accompanying haziness disappeared the island could no longer be seen. It had been utterly destroyed as well as its pirate inhabitants.[16]

The only river accounts of the 23 January shocks concerned the Ohio, at Louisville. The river had been frozen for several days, but on the twenty-second the ice began to break up, tumbling down the falls below the town with grinding crunch and resounding crash. Boats waiting at Louisville, and those at Shippingport a few miles downstream, had been trapped by the onset of winter ice. The crews of these vessels began to make their preparations for proceeding down the river. At seven in the morning of the twenty-third, the earthquake returned with a violence equal to the shock of

16. Myron L. Fuller, "The New Madrid Earthquake," U.S. Geological Survey *Bulletin* 494 (Washington: Government Printing Office, 1912):43. Stack or Crow's Nest Island had long been used by rogues of every description, including for a while the notorious pirate Samuel Mason. Otto A. Rothert, *The Outlaws of Cave-in-Rock* (Cleveland: Arthur A. Clark Co., 1924), pp. 202–3. Number thirty-two, said Cramer, was "destroyed by earthquake." He was less categorical about number ninety-four; it was "sunk by the earthquake or swept off by the floods." Cramer, *The Navigator,* pp. 180, 189.

the sixteenth and "much of the same character," according to Jared Brooks. But the demands of commerce were not to be postponed, and seven boats navigated the falls that day, with more preparing to follow. One foolhardy crew made the attempt at night. Brooks listened helplessly to the "howling and lamentation" of cries drifting up from the river, among them those of women and children. Boats that left Louisville and Shippingport at this time arrived in the general vicinity of New Madrid on the eve of the third great series of earthquakes.[17]

Among those departing was Vincent Nolte, a New Orleans merchant, who had more unlikely experiences in his long lifetime than the hero of a historical romance. He conversed with Napoleon, Victoria, Lafayette, and a host of lesser notables; arranged the conversion of a loan to the Papal states; fought with Jackson at New Orleans; served as the confidential adviser of an Austrian premier and as commissary for Louis Philippe; intrigued with Nicholas Biddle; and won and lost several fortunes. Inevitably, he witnessed the earthquakes at New Madrid.[18]

He left Shippingport in the company of twenty boats and tied up at New Madrid on 6 February, his head full of politics and the pending war with Great Britain (most of his crew was comprised of deep-water sailors who had left the idle ports of the eastern maritime towns to find work in Pittsburgh). He was awake in the early morning hours sketching a caricature of President Madison—depicting him in a general's uniform with his wife beside him in trousers, armed with a musket—when the earthquake struck. In the

17. Henry McMurtrie, *Sketches of Louisville and Its Environs* (Louisville: S. Penn, 1819), pp. 236–37; Nolte, *Fifty Years in Both Hemispheres,* pp. 180–81.
18. Nolte, *Fifty Years in Both Hemispheres,* pp. xxi–xxii.

confusion that followed Nolte kept his head. The crews of the other boats of the company cut their mooring lines and let the river take them. "I at once reflected that if, under the usual circumstances, it was dangerous, and therefore by no means advisable, to trust to the stream in the night, it must now be much more so, when the danger was greatly increased . . . and that consequently it would be a better plan to remain where we were until daylight." When he eventually reached Natchez he learned that "nothing was ever afterwards heard" of the boats that had been cast off so hastily.[19]

The fate of those boats was explained in an account written sometime later that accurately described the action of the river during the few hours after the first shock.

The current of the Mississippi, . . . was driven back upon its source with the greatest velocity for several hours, in consequence of an elevation of its bed. But this noble river was not thus to be stayed in its course. Its accumulated waters came booming on, and o'er topping the barrier thus suddenly raised, carried everything before them with resistless power. Boats, then floating on its surface, shot down the declivity like an arrow from a bow, amid roaring billows and the wildest commotion.[20]

No testimony by witnesses of this dramatic thrust upward of the river's bed below New Madrid has survived. But the effects of this action were widely observed and commented upon. Some narratives insisted that the river's current was pushed back upon itself. Bryan spoke of a "retrograde current, rapid as a torrent." From the appearance of the trees on the bank, James McBride, who passed the area in March, had no doubt that "the river at this place for some time ran up

19. Ibid., pp. 182–83.
20. Alphonso Wetmore, *Gazetteer of the State of Missouri* (St. Louis: C. Keemle, 1837), pp. 139–40.

stream with great velocity."[21] Even more compelling was the eyewitness account of Mathias Speed. His two boats strung together were tied up on the west bank opposite island number nine, a distance of twenty miles above New Madrid, when the first shock came. Forced to get underway by the imminent collapse of the bank, he had the good fortune to survive the hours of darkness. At daylight he saw island number ten before him and realized that he had come a distance of only four miles since three o'clock, "from which circumstance, and from that of an immense quantity of water rushing into the river from the woods—it is evident that the earth at this place, or below, had been raised so high as to stop the progress of the river, and caused it to overflow its banks."[22] The force of this recession was so great at New Madrid that "whole groves of young cotton-wood trees" were swept away. "They were broken off with such regularity, in some instances, that persons who had not witnessed the fact, would be [with] difficulty persuaded, that it has not been the work of art."[23]

When the river pushed itself over the barrier created by the elevation of its bed it left behind two sets of falls, the first a half mile above New Madrid and the second about eight miles downriver from the town. As Speed and his crew passed through the channel formed by island number ten

we were affrightened with the appearance of a dreadful rapid of falls in the river just below us; we were so far in the suck that it was impossible now to land—all hopes of surviving was [sic] now lost and certain destruction appeared to await us!

21. Dow, *History of Cosmopolite,* pp. 344–45; James McBride, "Brief Accounts of Journies in the Western Country, 1809–1812," *Quarterly Publication of the Historical and Philosophical Society of Ohio* 5:1 (January–March 1910):28.

22. Philadelphia *Pennsylvania Gazette,* 18 March 1812.

23. Dow, *History of Cosmopolite,* p. 345.

View of Long Reach
Ten miles long, beginning about thirty miles below Little Prairie, the
Long Reach ran by islands number twenty-five and twenty-six.
Cramer described it as "one of the most dangerous places between
New Orleans and the Ohio." Georges Henri Victor Collot, *A Journey in North America, Atlas* (Paris: Printed for Arthus Bertrand,
Bookseller, 1826), pl. 15. Courtesy of the Edward E. Ayer Collection, The Newberry Library, Chicago, Ill.

We . . . passed the rapids without injury, keeping our bow foremost, both boats being still lashed together.[24]

The crew of a boat approaching from behind was so alarmed that the men abandoned their boat and cargo and hastily put ashore in a canoe before they could be caught in the rapid current, making their way to the town overland.[25]

Both falls were estimated to be the size of the falls of the Ohio, a twenty-three-foot descent over a distance of two miles. The roar of the lower falls, although eight miles away, could be heard distinctly at New Madrid. As predicted in the Bardstown account, however, the soft sand and mud of the river's bottom was leveled in a few days, and the falls were eliminated. James Smith's letter to *The Navigator,* dated 18 February, made no mention of falls, although it was concerned chiefly with navigational hazards.[26]

For the most part the falls have been ignored by historical and scientific accounts of the earthquakes, although they were obviously supporting evidence for a dramatic event, the rising of the river's bed. The most important of these studies, published in 1912 by Myron Fuller of the United States Geological Survey, hardly mentioned the falls. Evidence for the falls and satisfactory evidence for the temporary reversal of the current appeared in the newspapers, which have been largely unexamined. The standard primary sources, which were mostly cumulative and written years after the event, did not mention the falls. These narrators, such

24. Philadelphia *Pennsylvania Gazette,* 18 March 1812.

25. Ibid.

26. Ibid., and 25 February 1812; Estwick Evans, *A Pedestrious Tour* (Concord, N.H.: Joseph C. Spear, 1819), p. 154; "Bardstown Letter"; "The falls had worn away to smooth rapids" by 20 February: Mitchill, "Detailed Narrative," pp. 301–2. Also, Fuller, "New Madrid Earthquake," pp. 90–91.

as Bryan, Lesieur, and Flint, emphasized that the river flowed backward for a time. But Fuller, relying upon these sources, had little to say about it and must have viewed the claim with considerable suspicion. More popular accounts have tended to seize upon the story rather too readily, and breathlessly introduce the day the laws of nature were suspended and the river reversed its current.[27]

The reversal of the current has often been grossly exaggerated and the time involved lengthened from a few hours to several days. L. Don Leet, a Harvard University seismologist, attributed the tale of the river flowing upstream "for three days and nights" to the "hysteria and superstition [of] on-the-spot reports." He believed the legend had its origin in the tidal-wave effect caused locally by the caving of the banks. This was true of 16 December, but the "on-the-spot reports," in contrast to the cumulative accounts, described a reversal on 7 February the scale and duration of which were not easily attributable to a few landslides. The question of chronology was important. There was a popular story that the *New Orleans,* the first steamboat to navigate western waters, while a few miles below the Ohio junction, found itself headed upstream—despite the thrust of its engines and a course set for Natchez.[28] The *New Orleans* experienced the shocks beginning on 16 December but had reached its destination long before 7 February. Only the newspaper accounts of eyewitnesses make it possible to distinguish the chronology of the earthquakes, and a chronology is essential to

27. Fuller, "New Madrid Earthquake," pp. 90–91; B. Clark, "America's Greatest Earthquake," *Reader's Digest* 94 (April 1969):110–14.

28. "North America's Most Violent Quake," *Natural History* 59 (February 1950):49–50.

establish that the rise of the bed and the reversal of the current were associated with the events of 7 February.

The skeptical reception of the story of the current's reversal led James MacFarlane, a nineteenth-century scientist anxious not to be taken in by popular legends, to insist that the earthquakes had never occurred. In a paper delivered in 1883 to the American Association for the Advancement of Science, he argued that the enormous tract extending from western Tennessee through southeastern Missouri and northeastern Arkansas, known as the "sunk lands," was formed when an underlying strata of limestone dissolved and the surface settled. MacFarlane caused a brief flurry in scientific circles. Much of the debate centered on the case of Reelfoot Lake, an eighteen-mile-long body of water to the east of New Madrid, created in western Tennessee by the earthquakes. Subsidence seemed a logical explanation for its formation. But inadvertently MacFarlane had wandered into the uncertain thickets of folklore. Local legend included the belief that the site, once the floor of a forest, had been the roof of a cavern that collapsed, making the depression of the lake. At Union City ten miles away, buildings in MacFarlane's time quaked when trains passed by, alarming the citizens who believed they resided over a cavern similar to the one that collapsed beneath Reelfoot.[29]

Partly in answer to MacFarlane, a government scientist of formidable repute named W J McGee presented

29. James MacFarlane, "The 'Earthquake' at New Madrid, Missouri, in 1811, Probably Not an Earthquake," *Proceedings of the American Association for the Advancement of Science* 32 (August 1883):247–48; "Discussion of MacFarlane's Paper," *Science* 2:31 (7 September 1883):324; W. F. Switzler, *Switzler's Illustrated History of Missouri from 1541 to 1877* (St. Louis: C. R. Burns, 1879), p. 185.

a paper in 1892 that attempted to prove that the Tiptonville Dome, so named for a town near its center in Lake County, Tennessee, was the result of a sudden uplift caused by the earthquakes. From this he drew certain conclusions:

The Lake county dome lies athwart the course of the Mississippi, which is here well out in the flood-plain; so that, if the lifting was effected suddenly, the flow of the river must have been obstructed. Now the declivity of the lower Mississippi is so slight and the land so low that the back water due to any obstruction spreads over an enormous area and reaches a vast volume; moreover, under the hypothesis, the Reelfoot lake depression was formed contemporaneously and the lake must have been filled by the water of the river taken not simply above the obstruction but . . . from many miles above. . . . Accordingly it may be considered certain that an immediate effect of the earthquake must have been a reversal of the flow of the Mississippi about what is now the northern extremity of Lake county, at least for many hours.[30]

Fuller agreed cautiously that some of the dome had been produced by the earthquakes, although he argued that most of it had been formed by earlier disturbances.[31] Neither Fuller nor McGee assigned a date to that part formed by the 1812 earthquakes. Probably McGee exaggerated the role of the river in creating Reelfoot. While it is not unlikely that the depression was flooded by the river, the lake, as David Dale Owen demonstrated long ago, was the result of a sand blow near the mouth of Reelfoot Creek, which, "being thereby dammed off, spread its waters over the adjacent low grounds, forming an extensive lake. . . . The deflected waters . . . turned their course to the south, and emptied into Obion river."[32] Nevertheless,

30. W J McGee, "A Fossil Earthquake," *Bulletin of the Geological Society of America* 4 (28 December 1892):411–14.
31. Fuller, "New Madrid Earthquake," p. 63.
32. David Dale Owen, *Report of the Geological Survey in Kentucky,*

McGee's basic hypothesis, the sudden uplift and the interference with the river's flow, was confirmed by the accounts of eyewitnesses, which make it possible to establish a date for the events.

About ten miles long north and south, the lower end of the Tiptonville Dome touches the lower end of Reelfoot. The bed at this end of the lake, higher than the upper end, is actually part of the uplift of the dome.[33] The upper part of the dome includes all of the New Madrid bend except for a substantial area at the tip across from the town. Below the town where it crosses into Missouri a short distance, the river has cut a path through it. Here the banks are higher than the surrounding alluvial plain.

From the earlier reconstruction of the events of 7 February, it is clear that the bed was obstructed at at least two places above and below the town, possibly as a result of activity in and around the dome, which, although it existed prior to 1812, according to Fuller experienced some additional uplift. The first obstruction, below the town, produced the effects on the river noticed at New Madrid. Bryan's account must have contributed markedly to the subsequent skeptical reception of the story that the current reversed itself for several hours. She said the river fell "immediately" after its first torrential backward flow. Although this might have appeared to result from the collapse of banks, the sudden recession could also be taken as an indirect indication that the river quickly surmounted the obstacle below the town, wearing it down to the falls, the roaring of which could be heard distinctly at New Madrid after daylight. Above the town, the story was more

Made during the Years 1854 and 1855, vol. 1 (Frankfort, Ky.: A. G. Hodges, Printer, 1856–1861), p. 117.

33. Fuller, "New Madrid Earthquake," p. 75.

clear-cut. In the dark Speed drifted for hours on a sluggish current, making little headway. At sunrise he watched the waters cascade from the banks as the river settled again into its channel, when his boat, caught in the grip of rapid water, dipped with terrifying abruptness into the declivity of the falls. Speed's own judgment, that the bed of the river had been raised to obstruct the river's course, cannot be lightly disregarded, and given the time element in his account, the obstruction must have been present for several hours.[34]

As chance would have it the first steamboat to navigate western waters—a dubious undertaking fraught with many difficulties in the best of circumstances—was being steered through this turbulence. No account of the earthquakes on the river would be complete without reference to this dramatic voyage.

The enterprise had been long in the making. The use of steamboats for river commerce was begun on the Hudson by Robert Fulton and Robert Livingston in 1807 and 1808 and in 1809 by John Stevens on the Delaware, but the applicability of this achievement for western waters remained in doubt. To insure a return on their investment capitalists demanded monopoly rights that state and territorial legislatures in the west were reluctant to grant. Earlier attempts had not been encouraging. John Fitch had failed before his grant of exclusive rights from Virginia had expired. Oliver Evans had built a boat at New Orleans, but before it was launched a flood carried it so far inland that it was found impractical to haul it back to the river, and the engine eventually powered a sawmill. When the Fulton-Livingston group wrung a concession of exclusive rights from the Territory of Orleans after failing with the

34. Dow, *History of Cosmopolite*, p. 345; Mitchill, "Detailed Narrative," pp. 300–301; Philadelphia *Pennsylvania Gazette*, 18 March 1812; Fuller, "New Madrid Earthquake," p. 63.

legislatures of Upper Louisiana and the Ohio Valley, westerners were concerned mainly with the infringement of the hard-won right of free navigation on the Mississippi and were hostile or indifferent to the enterprise itself.[35]

The success of the first voyage of the *New Orleans* was almost entirely attributable to the resourcefulness of Nicholas Roosevelt, an associate of Robert Fulton and Robert Livingston with a background as a mechanic and iron founder, who undertook a reconnaissance of the western rivers in 1810. With his wife, Lydia Latrobe Roosevelt, he lived aboard a flatboat for six months, interviewed boatmen and pilots from Pittsburgh to New Orleans, and studied the behavior of the rivers and the velocity of the current in all seasons. This preparation more than anything else was the key to his ultimate success. All that planning and foresight could accomplish went into his final report to Livingston and Fulton. In the end it gave him the margin needed to overcome even the earthquakes, an act of God no amount of planning could have foreseen. In the spring of 1811 he returned to Pittsburgh, armored with the financial support of his associates, to build a steamboat.[36]

The boat was built entirely of timber from the surrounding forests and the iron for the engine came from a local foundry; only the shipbuilder and mechanics to assemble the engine were brought from the east. They built what Bradbury, who boarded her at Natchez, called a "very handsome vessel," although it was proba-

35. Louis C. Hunter and Beatrice Jones Hunter, *Steamboats on the Western Rivers: An Economic and Technological History* (Cambridge: Harvard University Press, 1949), pp. 5–10.

36. J. H. B. Latrobe, *The First Steamboat Voyage on the Western Waters* (Baltimore: John Murphy, Printer, 1871), pp. 6–9; Charles Joseph Latrobe, *The Rambler in North America,* vol. 1 (London: R. B. Seeley and W. Burnside, 1835), pp. 104–5.

The *New Orleans*
James T. Lloyd, *Lloyd's Steamboat Directory and Disasters on the Western Waters* (Cincinnati: J. T. Lloyd and Co., 1856), p. 42, provided by The State Historical Society of Missouri, Columbia, Mo.

SCATTERGOOD Sc

bly closer in appearance to Noah's Ark than to later sternwheelers. One hundred and sixteen feet in length, with a twenty-foot beam, it disbursed a burden of 410 tons and mounted a thirty-four-cylinder engine.[37] In late September the trials had been run and the boat was ready to begin its historic voyage. The crew and passengers included, besides Roosevelt, a pregnant Lydia, a pilot, an engineer, six hands, two female servants, a cook, a messboy, and a large Newfoundland dog. To dramatize the speed of the vessel Roosevelt spurned the practice of stopping at sundown, preferring, whenever visibility permitted, to run all night.

The *New Orleans*'s sudden appearance on the river was met with awe and consternation. Above Cincinnati a young boy watched it round a bend, belching a cloud of steam, and raced home shouting, "The British are coming."[38] At Louisville on 1 October its midnight arrival in a shower of sparks and hissing steam caused many there to fear the comet had fallen into the broad Ohio. There Roosevelt waited six long weeks for a rise in the river in order to pass over the falls. During that time his wife gave birth, and the vessel returned briefly to Cincinnati to convince the skeptical citizens there and at Louisville that it could run against the current. Not until mid-December did the river rise.

The first shock of the earthquake noticed on board the boat occurred while it lay at anchor after passing the falls. "The effect was as though the vessel had been in motion and had suddenly grounded." But the shocks were never noticeable while the boat was underway. The clattering pistons, jarring machinery, and steady

37. Reuben Gold Thwaites, ed., *Early Western Travels, 1748–1846,* vol. 5: *Bradbury's Travels in the Interior of America, 1809–1811* (Cleveland: Arthur H. Clark Co., 1904), p. 211; J. H. B. Latrobe, *The First Steamboat Voyage,* pp. 11–12.

38. Leahy, *Who's Who on the Ohio River,* p. 312.

crump of the wheel muffled other sounds and disturbances. On shore they could see the trees "waving and
nodding . . . without a wind." At the mouth of the Ohio
they found the Mississippi swollen and turbid. They
stopped briefly at New Madrid and again, at Little
Prairie, "were bro't to by the cries of more of the
people." But at neither place did they take on passengers. Some indeed did wish to escape aboard, but
others were more fearful of the steamboat than of the
earthquakes. The caving of the banks began to be noticed "some distance below Little Prairie." It was here,
too, that the pilot became increasingly confused, finally
throwing up his hands in despair. The normal markers
of his trade, a tall tree here, the shape of an island there,
were gone. They followed the example of other boats
and stayed where the current was strongest.[39]

Each afternoon the boat pulled to the shore to allow
the crew to cut fuel.

Going ashore for wood . . . was looked forward to by the crew
with satisfaction, notwithstanding the labor that it involved.
And yet the men, if not sullenly, toiled silently; and if the
earth shook, as it often did, while they were at work, the
uplifted axe was suspended, or placed quietly on the log, and
the men stared at each other until it ceased.[40]

This silence prevailed on board also. "No one seemed
disposed to talk." The great dog "prowled about, moan-
ing and growling," but when he placed his head on
Lydia's lap, "it was a sure sign of a commotion of more
than usual violence."[41]

As the steamboat passed through the earthquake
zone the crew abandoned the night run and tied up

39. J. H. B. Latrobe, *The First Steamboat Voyage*, pp. 22– 23, 26;
Charles Joseph Latrobe, *Rambler in North America*, p. 108; St. Louis
Louisiana Gazette, 22 February 1812.
40. J. H. B. Latrobe, *The First Steamboat Voyage*, p. 27.
41. Ibid., pp. 26– 27.

instead. But they avoided the banks, for obvious reasons, and tied up at the downstream end of islands. According to one narrative they moored at one of the two islands that sunk, awakening in the morning to find it "had disappeared" and that the hawser, now straight down from the bow, had to be cut.[42] The *New Orleans* arrived in Natchez on 2 January, having come a distance of two thousand miles in less than ten days cruising time.

42. Ibid., p. 29; St. Louis *Louisiana Gazette,* 22 February 1812; probably island number thirty-two.

4. A Description of Damage

Every valley shall be exalted, and every mountain and hill shall be made low.

Isaiah (40:4)

Hills had disappeared, and lakes were found in their stead; and numerous lakes became elevated ground, over the surface of which vast heaps of sand were scattered in every direction, while in many places the earth for miles was sunk below the general level of the surrounding country, without being covered with water, leaving an *impression in miniature of a catastrophe much more important in its effects, which had, perhaps, preceded it ages before.*

Lewis F. Linn (1836)

The earthquake's epicentral zone encompassed southeastern Missouri and northeastern Arkansas. Topographically, this region was unlike any other part of the territory. Taken as a whole, the area was characterized by a series of lowland beds or bottomlands divided from one another by ridges running in a southern and in some cases a western direction. Some of this bottomland was poorly drained or even undrained, but these wet areas were not true swamps, since a sandy alluvium could be reached only a few inches below the rotting vegetation. There was enough drainage to permit farming, however, and the soil was exceedingly fertile. The ridges dividing the bottomlands were remnants of what had been a continuous surface until ero-

A Description of Damage

Riverbanks Falling In
—Missouri River
Courtesy of The State
Historical Society of Missouri, Columbia, Mo.

sion formed the beds between them. The largest and most important of these was Crowley Ridge, which arose at a point thirty-five miles west of the Ohio junction. Only its northern portion was in Missouri; it stretched one hundred miles further into Arkansas. Another ridge was the formation that ended at New Madrid, where it touched the river and formed the high banks of the townsite. The beds between these and other ridges were in reality former channels of the Mississippi, dating from a time when the river followed and later abandoned paths west of its present route. In other words, the fundamental topography of the region was formed by the action of the river—indeed, the rivers, since the Ohio once joined the Mississippi south of its present point of entry—and not by the earthquakes, although the latter is a common misconception.[1]

Two accounts highlight the difficulty of distinguishing between the action of the rivers and the earthquakes as forces that shaped the region. The first of these, by Amos Stoddard, was a volume completed just before the earthquakes for the purpose of presenting the advantages and disadvantages (with an emphasis on the former) of the region bordering the Mississippi in the Louisiana Purchase. The second, a letter dated 1 February 1836 from Missouri Sen. Lewis F. Linn to the Senate Committee on Commerce, had the political purpose of encouraging federal assistance for the draining of the region. Consequently, he emphasized the potential wealth of its agricultural resources as well as its enormous mineral deposits, the development of which was blocked by peculiar but

1. C. F. Marbut, "The Evolution of the Northern Part of the Lowlands of Southeastern Missouri," *University of Missouri Studies* 1:3 (July 1902): 1–63.

correctable conditions that Linn said were caused by the earthquakes.

Linn's opinion was one often met with in later accounts. Using Godfrey Lesieur as his source, Linn described the scars left by the disaster but insisted that they gave "an *impression in miniature of a catastrophe much more important in its effects, which had, perhaps, preceded it ages before.*"[2] This impression he sought to counter by attributing basic topographical features to the earthquakes. Thus he argued that the "great swamp" beginning "two or three miles" below Cape Girardeau had once been the bed of a river, either the Mississippi or the St. Francis augmented by the waters of the Castor and Little rivers, the channel of which was abandoned in 1812 because of the convulsions. Of the ridges separating the bottomlands—the " 'cote sans dessein,' or hills without design" of the French—he speculated

that the far greater portion of this gloomy region, annually covered by water, and at all seasons by a heavy growth of timber, and thick canebrakes, closely interwoven by many plants of the convolvulous order, was *once* high ground, but during some convulsion of nature sunk to its present general level, leaving spots unaffected to tower in grandeur over the surrounding scene of desolation.[3]

That "convulsion of nature" he identified as the earthquakes.

Two portions of Stoddard's description of the region were relevant to this discussion. In the first he discussed its general healthfulness.

The tract of country . . . between the Arkansas and Tiwappaty bottom [an area stretching from north of New Madrid to

2. Alphonso Wetmore, *Gazetteer of the State of Missouri* (St. Louis: C. Keemle, 1837), p. 140.
3. Ibid., p. 139.

twelve miles or so south of Cape Girardeau], is more insalubrious than any other part of Upper Louisiana; and from the situation of it a stranger would be inclined to believe, that it was more subject to dangerous diseases than it really is. Complaints of an epidemic nature, are unknown. Deaths are more frequent among children than adults; and this is imputed to the green fruit, which the former indulge themselves in eating during the most sickly season of the year. The mephitic exhalations from the swamps and low grounds must necessarily poison the air; they produce intermittents, and some bilious fevers, though they have never been considered as very malignant. Indeed, the sick have suffered more from the want of medicine than from the obstinate nature of the endemics; and more mortality has occurred from old age and accidents than from prevalent diseases.[4]

Stoddard was facing objections often raised to the settlement of the region in a way that revealed that its appearance more than justified the objections. Although Stoddard was too good a reporter to gloss over the disadvantages, he did the best he could to strike a balance.

The river St. Francis runs nearly parallel to the Mississippi, and from thirty to forty miles, (in some places less) to the westward of it, for the distance of about four hundred and sixty miles, and mostly through the flat country already mentioned. Nearly half of the lands between these two rivers are covered with swamps and ponds, and periodically inundated. These swamps, filled with cypress, are mostly dry in summer; though, unless they be drained at great expense, or banks constructed to keep the water from them, they will never be of any service to agriculturalists, other than as ranges for cattle. Many creeks or bayous take their rise in them, and they flow into both rivers; and it is calculated, that there are as many of them as one to every fifteen miles. These swamps are generally in a central position between the two rivers; they

4. Amos Stoddard, *Sketches, Historical and Descriptive, of Louisiana* (Philadelphia: Mathew Carey, 1812), p. 210.

mostly communicate with both by forming creeks or bayous, which are navigable in the time of freshes.[5]

Although Stoddard emphasized the extensive tracts of prairie and forest and their potential agricultural value, his description overall left little room to doubt that many of the characteristic features of the region later attributed to the earthquakes were already present. In particular, before the disaster of 1811–1812 it had earned a deserved reputation as the "sunk country."

Even so, it remained abundantly clear that damage to the surface as a result of the earthquakes was extensive, disastrous, and varied. Much land was sunk; lakes and ponds were formed, and the courses of rivers and streams were changed; other land was uplifted. Fissures, sand blows, and extrusions of various kinds were common. Trees, sometimes entire forests, were damaged in a variety of ways. Finally, this scarring of the surface was often accompanied, as might be expected in a region so poorly drained, by widespread flooding.

Land along the banks of the Mississippi sank conspicuously at several places—New Madrid, Little Prairie, and Big Prairie all occupied sites affected in this way—and the many reports from boatmen indicated the channel was at times significantly altered. There were also numerous references to changes in the courses of other streams and rivers. One witness, for instance, said the "Saint Francois ... intirely [sic] changed its bed for a long distance up." North and south of the Arkansas line this river wandered through what Linn called "lagoons" and "slimy quagmires" to form a lake as extensive as Reelfoot and with many of the same features, including sunken forests.[6]

5. Ibid., p. 208.
6. St. Louis *Louisiana Gazette*, 22 February 1812 and 7 March 1812; Thomas Nuttall, *A Journal of Travels into the Arkansa Territory*,

The sinking of large tracts of forest, whether subsequently submerged or not, was among the more impressive sights left behind by the earthquakes. An account from Tennessee reported that eighteen to twenty acres near Piney River had sunk so low "that the tops of the trees were on a level with the surrounding earth." On the Illinois side of the Ohio River, near Paducah, Kentucky, a circular basin one hundred feet in diameter sank in the midst of a tract of post-oaks, leaving the tops of the tallest trees below the surface.[7]

As an example of land sunk by the earthquakes, Reelfoot Lake in western Tennessee has always stirred popular imagination and attracted scientific attention. Its existence was mute confirmation of the power of the earthquakes. Its scale made it the most characteristic of the sunken lands and provided an opportunity for scientists to study the phenomenon in its most perfect form. Reelfoot first appeared in the sources in Bryan's letter, where it was described as a lake formed in the Indian country "upwards of one hundred miles in length." In 1836 Linn gave its depth as fifty to one hundred feet. In fact, it was eighteen miles long, up to five miles wide, and five to twenty feet deep. Its bottom was often described in popular literature as the former floor of "a luxuriant forest coursed by little streams of

vol. 63 (Ann Arbor: University Microfilms, 1966), p. 58; Clarence Edwin Carter, ed., *Territorial Papers of the United States,* vol. 14: *Louisiana–Missouri, 1806–1814* (Washington: Government Printing Office, 1949), pp. 591, 624; Timothy Dudley, "The Earthquake of 1811 at New Madrid, Missouri (from the Narrative of an Eyewitness)," *Annual Report of the Board of Regents of the Smithsonian Institution . . . for the Year 1858* (Washington: William A. Harris, Printer, 1859), p. 422; Louis Bringier, "Notices of the Geology, Mineralogy, Topography, Production, and Aboriginal Inhabitants of the Regions around the Mississippi and Its Confluent Waters," *American Journal of Science and Arts* 3 (1821):22.

7. Philadelphia *Pennsylvania Gazette,* 5 February 1812; Dudley, "The Earthquake of 1811," p. 423.

water," but in fact it was mostly low and swampy before the earthquakes; the predominating timber was cypress, and in 1912 Myron Fuller could still make out the outlines of the basins that had once been Mississippi sloughs. However, many of the dead trees that projected starkly above the surface of the water were walnut, ash, oak, mulberry, and other varieties common to higher and drier ground.[8]

The reverse of the process forming Reelfoot occurred also, and many areas were uplifted. The largest and most impressive formations were the domes. Fuller identified two besides Tiptonville, both in Arkansas: Blytheville Dome, near the Missouri line with a seven-to-ten-mile radius, and the much smaller Little River Dome west of the St. Francis River.[9] There were numerous examples of uplifting on a smaller scale. One witness, who saw something of the country west of the Mississippi after the 16 December shocks, left a vivid description:

The most extraordinary effect that I saw was a small lake below the river St. Francis. The bottom of which is blown up higher than any of the adjoining country, and instead of water it is filled with a beautiful white sand. The same effect is produced in many other lakes. . . . A little river called

8. Lorenzo Dow, *History of Cosmopolite; or, the Four Volumes of Lorenzo Dow's Journal* (Wheeling, Va.: Joshua Martin, 1848), p. 345; Wetmore, *Gazetteer of Missouri*, p. 140; Myron L. Fuller, "The New Madrid Earthquake," U.S. Geological Survey *Bulletin* 494 (Washington: Government Printing Office, 1912):73–74; Fuller said the length of Reelfoot was eight or ten miles. David Dale Owen, *Report of the Geological Survey in Kentucky, Made during the Years 1854 and 1855,* vol. 1 (Frankfort, Ky.: A. G. Hodges, Printer, 1856–1861), p. 117; Federal Writer's Project, *Tennessee: A Guide to the State* (New York: Viking Press, 1939), p. 429.

9. Fuller, "New Madrid Earthquake," pp. 63–64. According to Fuller, Tiptonville and Little River domes were formed partially by the 1811–1812 earthquakes and partially by earlier disturbances, but Blytheville Dome was formed earlier and "did not result from the shock of 1811."

A Description of Damage

Distant View of Reelfoot Lake
David Dale Owen, *Report of the Geological Survey in Kentucky, Made during the Years 1854 and 1855,* in 4 vols., vol. 1 (Frankfort, Ky., 1856–1861), pl. 117. Courtesy of The Joseph Regenstein Library, University of Chicago.

Pemisece [Pemiscot], that empties into St. Francis, and runs parallel with the Mississippi, at the distance of about twelve miles from it, is filled also with sand. I only saw it near its bend, and found it to be so, and was informed by respectable gentlemen who had seen it lower down, that it was positively filled with sand. On the sand that was thrown out of the lakes and river lie numerous quantities of fish of all kinds common to the country.[10]

Another account said the Pemiscot "blew up for a distance of nearly fifty miles."[11]

In at least one case a slough was raised. Sloughs were pockets formed as the river altered its course, which, in time, became severed entirely from the stream. Gradually they filled with sediment from flood waters. Cypresses encircled them, with the older trees in the outer circle and the younger ones toward the center as they filled, and swamps were formed. On the Tennessee side at the entrance to the New Madrid bend between the river and Reelfoot Lake, a domelike expanse of ground, regular in shape, "looking as if when soft it had been pressed up from beneath," was described in 1837. At that time it was a "beautiful piece of land . . . now high and dry . . . covered with a uniform growth of young cottonwood," although it sat in the midst of a canebrake. It was identified as a former slough by the cypresses encircling it.[12]

Of all the phenomena of the earthquakes none filled people with more fascinated horror than fissuring. The dread of being swallowed by the earth and buried alive was captured by a somewhat later account of a scene at Little Prairie: "Here was a little cluster of men, with pale-visaged women and children holding on to their

10. *Pittsburgh Gazette,* 14 February 1812.
11. Dudley, "The Earthquake of 1811," pp. 421–22.
12. F. C. Usher, "On the Elevation of the Banks of the Mississippi in 1811," *American Journal of Science and Arts* 31 (January 1837):294–96.

skirts, gazing with spasmodic, open-mouthed wonder at a fearful chasm in the earth, out of which issued a current of steam, with serpent-like hissings."[13] Flint's story of the inhabitants clinging to trees stretched over the chasms also evoked the picture of a people threatened by yawning pits and saved only by their ingenuity. Despite the terror engendered by fissures, however, only one firsthand account described someone actually falling into one. Mathias Speed related the tale of a man marooned for several days on island number ten, just above New Madrid, following the shocks of 7 February.

The violent agitation of the ground was such at one time as induced him to hold to a tree to support himself; the earth gave way at the place, and he with the tree sunk down, and he got wounded in the fall. The fissure was so deep as to put it out of his power to get out at that place. He made his way along the fissure until a sloping slide offered him an opportunity of crawling out.[14]

The only thing known to be swallowed by a fissure that subsequently closed, assuming the story to be true, was a boatload of castings stored in a cellar that vanished without a trace.[15]

Fissuring did give rise to a number of bizarre anecdotes. One told of the old gentleman at Little Prairie who complained bitterly that fissuring had caused his well to move twenty yards from the spot where he had sunk it next to his cabin.[16] Another, attributed to Lesieur, concerned Culbertson's smokehouse:

One of the most remarkable incidents occurred ten miles below Little Prairie on Pemiscot River. An old man named

13. Wetmore, *Gazetteer of Missouri*, p. 132.

14. Philadelphia *Pennsylvania Gazette*, 18 March 1812.

15. John Wells Foster, *The Mississippi Valley: Its Physical Geography* (Chicago: S. C. Griggs and Co., 1869), p. 21.

16. Wetmore, *Gazetteer of Missouri*, pp. 132–33.

Culbertson with his family lived on a short bend in the river. About an acre of ground lay between his house and the river, and in this space was situated the well and smokehouse. On the morning of the 16th of December, after the second hard shock had subsided, Mrs. Culbertson started to the well for water and to the smokehouse for breakfast meat, when, to her great astonishment, no well or smokehouse was to be seen. Upon further search, they were both found on the opposite side of the river, and a canoe was necessary to reach them. The swelling of the earth had formed a fissure across the bend wide enough to permit the whole volume of the water to pass through, and the great pressure upon the point thus isolated forced it to the opposite bank, when the next land wave appeared.[17]

Myron Fuller identified two kinds of fissures in the earthquake zone, "one due to the down-faulting of narrow strips of earth, and the other to the cracking of the soil by tension as the earth waves progressed across the surface."[18] The first caused wide depressions but not the gaping chasms of the narratives. Those were created by the second type and produced the greatest alarm. In the words of Lesieur:

The earth was observed to be rolling in waves of a few feet in height, with a visible depression between. By and by these swells burst, throwing up large volumes of water, sand and a species of charcoal, some of which was partly covered with a substance, which by its peculiar odor was thought to be sulphur. When these swells burst, large, wide and long fissures were left.[19]

Fissuring occurred over an extensive range. There was a record of numerous "chasms in the earth" as far south as the mouth of the Arkansas River, nearly four hundred miles downstream from the entrance of the

17. *History of Southeast Missouri* (Chicago: Goodspeed Publishing Co., 1888), p. 307.
18. Fuller, "New Madrid Earthquake," p. 52.
19. R. A. Campbell, ed., *Campbell's Gazetteer of Missouri* (St. Louis: R. A. Campbell, 1874), pp. 394–95.

Ohio. To the north local fissuring occurred ninety miles up the Ohio from the junction with the Mississippi and about the same distance up the Mississippi. But it was in the zone of principal disturbance, in northeastern Arkansas and southeastern Missouri, that fissuring was most widespread. These cracks were a terrifying obstacle during the flight from New Madrid on the morning of 7 February. At Little Prairie, in March, James McBride found the "surface of the ground . . . cracked in almost every direction." These chasms were not the bottomless abysses imagined by the fearful observers; many were only a few inches wide and quite shallow. The deepest measured by Fuller was twenty feet. Hindsight is a comfortable way to assess the question, however. For those in the grip of events the desire to learn the accurate depth of fissures was assigned a low priority. "Their depth none knew, as no one had strength of nerve sufficient to fathom them."[20]

There was a discrepancy in the narratives on the subject of fissures. Lesieur, joined by Bryan, Flint, and others, insisted that material was ejected from fissures. As we have seen, Lesieur spoke of swells bursting and water, sand, and charcoal being thrown up. This was at variance with several other firsthand descriptions. Mathias Speed traveled overland from New Madrid after 7 February. He found numerous cracks in the earth but said explicitly: "Nothing appeared to have issued from the cracks but where there was sand and

20. Philadelphia *Pennsylvania Gazette,* 11 March 1812; Emil J. Mateker, "Earthquakes in Missouri," *Washington University Magazine* 39 (1968):51; John Shaw, "New Madrid Earthquake: Account of Colonel John Shaw," *Missouri Historical Review* 6 (January 1912):92; Dudley, "The Earthquake of 1811," p. 422; James McBride, "Brief Accounts of Journies in the Western Country, 1809–1812," *Quarterly Publication of the Historical and Philosophical Society of Ohio* 5:1 (January–March 1910):29; Fuller, "New Madrid Earthquake," p. 52.

stone coal, they seem to have been thrown up from holes; in most of those, which varied in size, there was water standing."[21] William Leigh Pierce, whose description of water spouts on the surface of the river has been quoted earlier, at one point went ashore on an island.

I was gratified with seeing several places where those spouts which had so much attracted our wonder and admiration had arisen; they were generally on the beach; and have left large circular holes in the sand, formed much like a funnel. For a great distance around the orifice, vast quantities of coal have been scattered, many pieces weighing from 15 to 20 lbs. were discharged 160 measured paces—These holes were of various dimensions; one of them I observed most particularly, it was 16 feet in perpendicular depth, and 63 feet in circumferences at the mouth.[22]

This association of ejected material with sand blows and not fissures was confirmed by other narratives.[23] But too many also insisted that extrusions occurred from fissures to be altogether disregarded. This is especially true of a number which described fissures opening, and then closing immediately, throwing "water, sand and

21. Campbell, *Gazetteer of Missouri*, pp. 394– 95; Dow, *History of Cosmopolite*, p. 345; quote in Philadelphia *Pennsylvania Gazette*, 18 March 1812.

22. *New York Evening Post*, 11 February 1812. For verification of the weight of coal chunks, see Winthrop Sargent, "Account of Several Shocks of an Earthquake in the Southern and Western Parts of the United States," *Memoirs of the American Academy of Arts and Sciences* 3:2 (1815):357.

23. McBride, "Brief Accounts," pp. 29– 30. One item ejected at some point was the fossil skull of an ox, subsequently named *Bos bombifrons*. In the cautious opinion of the scientist who described it, it "could not with propriety be referred to any animal at present existing within the limits of the United States" and so was held to be a new species. J. E. DeKay, "Notes on a Fossil Skull," New York Academy of Sciences *Annals of the Lyceum of Natural History* 2 (March 1826):280– 91, quote on p. 281.

mud, in high jets, higher than the tops of the trees."[24]

Damage to forests was extensive. Fuller estimated that 150,000 acres of timber had been destroyed, but a satisfactory total was beyond calculation. The region contained many tracts of deciduous trees, and observers were lavish in their descriptions of the effect of the earthquakes upon them. During the shocks "trees lashed their tops together," and in general "were violently agitated," falling "thousands at a time." Throughout the region reports were made of forests overthrown or of trees "standing inclined in every direction." Nor were forest trees the only victims; great damage was inflicted on orchards. One ten-acre orchard was destroyed on the banks of the Pemiscot. The sight of entire forests suddenly reduced to matchsticks usually inspired military metaphors. Cramer said that the wooded area next to Little Prairie looked "as if it had been in a desperate engagement, in which it got worsted." Another narrator observed entire "forests . . . fall prostrate . . . like soldiers grounding their arms." There were numerous instances of trees split up the center, "one part standing on one side of a fissure and the other part on the other." Lyell investigated one tract, "chiefly oaks and walnuts . . . , many of them 200 years old," which were "killed by the loosening of the roots during the repeated undulations." Many trees were left standing upright in the Mississippi. The tops of the trees of sunken island number thirty-two projected out of the water. Occasionally trees were left standing upright in the water when banks slid into the

24. Samuel Prescott Hildreth, "History of a Voyage from Marietta to New Orleans in 1805," *The American Pioneer* 1 (1842):130; Reuben Gold Thwaites, ed., *Early Western Travels, 1748–1846*, vol. 5: *Bradbury's Travels in the Interior of America, 1809–1811* (Cleveland: Arthur H. Clark Co., 1904), p. 209.

river; but usually the trees came crashing down, "tossing their arms to and fro, as if sensible of their danger."[25]

25. Fuller, "New Madrid Earthquake," p. 99; *Pittsburgh Gazette*, 31 January 1812; New Orleans *Louisiana Gazette and Daily Advertiser*, 31 December 1811; Zadok Cramer, *The Navigator*, 8th ed. (Pittsburgh: Cramer, Spear and Eichbaum, 1814), reprinted in Ethel C. Leahy, *Who's Who on the Ohio River and Its Tributaries* (Cincinnati: E. C. Leahy Publishing Co., 1931), pp. 178–79; Bringier, "Notices of the Geology," pp. 20–21; Edwin James, *Account of an Expedition from Pittsburgh to the Rocky Mountains*, vol. 65 (Ann Arbor: University Microfilms, 1966), p. 326; Dudley, "The Earthquake of 1811," pp. 421–23; Samuel Latham Mitchill, "A Detailed Narrative of the Earthquakes," *Transactions of the Literary and Philosophical Society of New York* 1 (1814):301; Foster, *The Mississippi Valley*, pp. 20–21; McBride, "Brief Accounts," p. 30; Sir Charles Lyell, *A Second Visit to the United States of North America*, vol. 2 (New York: Harper and Brothers Publishers, 1849), p. 178; *New York Evening Post*, 11 February 1812; Sargent, "Account of Several Shocks of an Earthquake," p. 355; Hildreth, "History of a Voyage," pp. 129–30.

5. Effects and Responses

Such are thy throes, O God of Nature!

Zadok Cramer

One person with a very serious face, told me, that when he was ousted from his bed, he was verily afraid, and thought the Day of Judgment had arrived, until he reflected that the Day of Judgment would not come in the night.

Anonymous

The night before the earthquakes began, the detached kitchen of a plantation in Livingston County, Kentucky, normally the center of routine domestic life, became a setting for horror. In the flickering light, terrified slaves watched their master slaughter a habitual runaway as an object lesson; then one of their number was handed the ax and told to dismember the corpse. Piece by piece, the bloody fragments were consigned to the fire. After the mess was cleaned up, witnesses and murderers departed to find what rest they could. The fire burned on, but before its work was finished, the ground quaked, the cabin rocked, and the fireplace collapsed into the hearth, smothering it. The unburnt fragments of bone were hidden in the masonry when the fireplace was rebuilt; but the quakes continued, and on 7 February the fireplace collapsed again. This time, a dog arrived before the repair crew. A neighbor later found it gnawing on the charred head of

EARTHQUAKE.

We have the following description of the Earthquake from gentlemen who were on board a large barge, and lay at anchor in the Mississippi a few leagues below New Madrid, on the night of the 15th of December. About 2 o'clok all hands were awakened by the first shock; the impression was, that the barge had dragged her anchor and was grounding on gravel; such were the feelings for 60 or 80 seconds, when the shock subsided. The crew were so fully persuaded of the fact of their being aground, that they put out their sounding poles, but found water enough.

At seven next morning a second and very severe shock took place. The barge was under way—the river rose several feet; the trees on the shore shook; the banks in large columns tumbled in; hundreds of old trees that had lain perhaps half a century at the bottom of the river, appeared on the surface of the water; the feathered race took to the wing; the canopy was covered with geese and ducks, and various other kinds of wild fowl; very little wind; the air was tainted with a nitrous and sulphureous smell; and every thing was truly alarming for several minutes. The shocks continued to the 21st Dec. during that time perhaps one hundred were distinctly felt. From the river St Francis to the Chickasaw bluffs visible marks of the earthquake were discovered; from that place down, the banks did not appear to have been disturbed.

There is one part of this description which we cannot reconcile with philosophic principles, (although we believe the narrative to be true,) that is, the trees which were settled at the bottom of the river appearing on the surface It must be obvious to every person that those trees must have become specifically heavier than the water before they sunk, and of course after being immersed in the mud must have increased in weight.— We therefore submit the question to the Philosophical Society.

From the New Orleans *Louisiana Gazette and Daily Advertiser,* 20 January 1812, p. 2. In the possession of the Elmer Ellis Library, University of Missouri, Columbia, Mo.

the victim and the dreadful secret was out. Two nephews of Thomas Jefferson, Lilburne and Isham Lewis, were indicted for the murder of Lilburne's slave George.[1]

The Livingston County episode was a consequence of the earthquakes. Though none were so bizarre, there were many others. In ways often special to their time and place, the creatures of the valley responded to the stress of the quake's sudden onslaught. As the shocks continued, there was also evidence of the effects of strain under conditions of prolonged stress. The responses, in most cases, did not await the arrival of a Kentucky dog. They were immediate and emphatic.

The Mississippi River was and is a major highway for migratory birds. Game and nongame varieties were settled in vast numbers in the sloughs and bayous of the lower river or were roosting in the trees of the surrounding forests when the earthquakes struck. When the shocks disturbed them, they raised an insistent clamor. Bradbury said "the screaming of the geese, and other wild-fowl, produced an idea that all nature was in a state of dissolution." Ducks, geese, "and various other kinds of wild fowl" settled on the boats, often blanketing an entire canopy. On shore the smaller birds "retreated to the bosoms of men," landed on heads and shoulders, and crowded about the "fires of those who had left their dwellings" seeking the company of known enemies rather than face the terror of the unknown alone. But all reports on the behavior of birds came from the early shocks, which suggests that they sought a more hospitable environment rather quickly.[2]

---

1. Lilburne killed himself, and Isham, also indicted as an accessory in the suicide, broke jail and disappeared. Boynton Merrill, Jr., *Jefferson's Nephews: A Frontier Tragedy* (Princeton, N.J.: Princeton University Press, 1976), pp. 256–302.

2. Reuben Gold Thwaites, ed., *Early Western Travels, 1748–*

The New Madrid Earthquakes

Reports from riders indicated that their horses seemed to have a few seconds' prior knowledge of the onset of shocks. John James Audubon wrote of riding through "the Barrens of Kentucky" when he noticed

a sudden and strange darkness rising from the western horizon. Accustomed to our heavy storms of thunder and rain I took no more notice of it, as I thought the speed of my horse might enable me to get under shelter of the roof of an acquaintance, who lived not far distant. . . . I had proceeded about a mile, when I heard what I imagined to be the distant rumbling of a violent tornado, on which I spurred my steed, with a wish to gallop as fast as possible to a place of shelter; but it would not do, the animal knew better than I what was forthcoming, and instead of going faster, so nearly stopped that I remarked he placed one foot after another on the ground, with as much precaution as if walking on a smooth sheet of ice. I thought he had suddenly foundered, and speaking to him, was on the point of dismounting and leading him, when he all of a sudden fell a-groaning piteously, hung his head, spread out his four legs, as if to save himself from falling, and stood stock still, continuing to groan. I thought my horse was about to die, and would have sprung from his back had a minute more elapsed, but at that instant all the shrubs and trees began to move from their very roots, the ground rose and fell in successive furrows, like the ruffled waters of a lake.[3]

_1846,_ vol. 5: _Bradbury's Travels in the Interior of America, 1809–1811_ (Cleveland: Arthur H. Clark Co., 1904), p. 208; Samuel Prescott Hildreth, "History of a Voyage from Marietta to New Orleans in 1805," _The American Pioneer_ 1 (1842):129–30; Lorenzo Dow, _History of Cosmopolite; or, the Four Volumes of Lorenzo Dow's Journal_ (Wheeling, Va.: Joshua Martin, 1848), p. 344; Maria R. Audubon, ed., _Audubon and His Journals_ (New York: Charles Scribner's Sons, 1897), pp. 236–37; _New York Evening Post,_ 11 February 1812; New Orleans _Louisiana Gazette and Daily Advertiser,_ 20 January 1812; Timothy Flint, _Recollections of the Last Ten Years_ (New York: Alfred A. Knopf, 1932), p. 216; Zadok Cramer, _The Navigator,_ 8th ed. (Pittsburgh: Cramer, Spear and Eichbaum, 1814), reprinted in Ethel C. Leahy, _Who's Who on the Ohio River and Its Tributaries_ (Cincinnati: E. C. Leahy Publishing Co., 1931), p. 178.

   3. Audubon, _Audubon and His Journals,_ pp. 234–35.

Other accounts reported the same behavior. Bringier said his horse "stood motionless, struck with a panic of terror." Another individual in Kentucky said his horse "refused to proceed, and bracing himself on his legs, stood still." Nolte, riding from Frankfort to Louisville when the 23 January shock struck, said his horse "as if struck by lightning, suddenly stood still."[4]

The behavior of wildlife during the shocks was noticed also.

One morning grandpop and grandmother, after having spent a sleepless night, in watching for the Coming of Death, which they hourly expected, as the grim dawn came down on the troubled world, beheld great wild animals in his [sic] yard and garden. There were bears, panthers, wolves, foxes, etc. side by side with a number of wild deer, with their red tongues hanging out of their mouths. There was no sign of

4. Louis Bringier, "Notices of the Geology, Mineralogy, Topography, Production, and Aboriginal Inhabitants of the Regions around the Mississippi and Its Confluent Waters," *American Journal of Science and Arts* 3 (1821):20; Samuel Latham Mitchill, "A Detailed Narrative of the Earthquakes," *Transactions of the Literary and Philosophical Society of New York* 1 (1814):298; Vincent Nolte, *Fifty Years in Both Hemispheres; or, Reminiscences of a Merchant's Life* (London: Trubner and Co., 1854), p. 180. According to Otto W. Nuttli, "the horse felt the P wave, or the first wave from the earthquake, whereas the rider felt the larger amplitude surface waves which would have arrived one or two minutes later." Wayne Viitanen, "The Winter the Mississippi Ran Backwards," *Register of the Kentucky Historical Society* 71 (January 1973):56. The animals' prior knowledge was a common observation. For instance, Deodatus de Dolomieu, a French geologist who investigated the Calabrian earthquake of 1783, said "the presentiment of animals at the approach of earthquakes, is a singular phenomenon, and which cannot fail to surprise us so much the more, as we know not by what organs it is communicated to them." *Encyclopaedia; or, a Dictionary of Arts, Sciences, and Miscellaneous Literature,* vol. 6 (Philadelphia: Thomas Dobson, Printer, 1798), p. 284. Compare Paul Reasenberg, "Unusual Animal Behavior Before Earthquakes," *Earthquake Information Bulletin* 10 (March–April 1978):42–48, and Shen Ling-huang, "Can Animals Help to Predict Earthquakes?" *Earthquake Information Bulletin* 10 (November–December 1978):231–33.

enmity, but all seemed animated by a common danger . . . nor did they seem to fear man.[5]

As bizarre as animal behavior seemed to be, the effect of the prolonged shocks on humans was far more complex. Over the course of several months violent shocks were felt in every period of the day, but a number of them were concentrated in the time between two and four o'clock in the morning. The onset of both the 16 December and the 7 February series occurred within that time. "As we were all wrapt in sleep," began a typical account, "each tells his story in his own way."[6]

The stories that each had to tell were repetitious in their agreement. In South Carolina "the earthquakes terrified the inhabitants exceedingly." "Great indeed was the consternation of the inhabitants," another account read. "People were heard to scream with terror" in the streets of New York. At South Carolina College "the students . . . left their chambers without their clothes" in the early morning hours of 16 December. Nearer the earthquake epicenters, according to Cramer, people felt "terror and alarm to a degree little short of madness." The paramount fear of those in the epicentral region was the imminent possibility of being swallowed by the earth. "Who can tell of the sensations which I experienced when I found myself rocking as it were on my horse, and with him moved to and fro like a child in a cradle . . . expecting the ground every moment to open and present to my eye such an abyss as might engulf myself and all around me?"[7]

5. Samuel M. McDaniel, "Journals and Diaries," manuscript in Missouri Historical Society archive, St. Louis, Mo.

6. St. Louis *Louisiana Gazette,* 21 December 1811.

7. Mitchill, "Detailed Narrative," pp. 284, 286; *New York Evening Post,* 26 December 1811, 22 February 1812; Cramer, *The Navigator,* p. 178; Audubon, *Audubon and His Journals,* p. 235; see also, *Pittsburgh Gazette,* 14 February 1812 and 21 February 1812.

Effects and Responses

Equilibrium was affected in many. In faraway Richmond, Virginia, people "staggered as they stood"; in Savannah, Georgia, they "were made to totter, as if on shipboard"; near Hodgenville, Kentucky, they felt light-headed and reeled about "like a drunken man." But in New Madrid they were "thrown on the ground at almost every step" during the violent shakes. Over the range and time period of the earthquakes a profile could be constructed of general and widespread physical symptoms resulting from the constant buffeting. These included giddiness, nausea, vomiting, debility, trembling knees, and pains in the knees and legs. Far from the center, where the shocks were less frequent, people were apt to attribute their symptoms to other, more prosaic causes. An individual in Baltimore thought that his gout had moved to his head, but his daughter blamed her faintness on the heat of the fire in the hearth. Physical symptoms were accompanied by psychological disorientation. Audubon confessed to becoming "bewildered" in his ideas.[8] Jared Brooks left this description:

Sound (as often of late) seems, as it were, to have lost its rotundity, and matter its sonorous properties—the peal of the bell, the beat of the drum, the crowing of the cock, the human call, although near at hand seem to be at a distance, and the different reports seem to steal, in a manner silently,

8. Mitchill, "Detailed Narrative," pp. 285, 286, 304; William Allen Pusey, "New Madrid Earthquake, an Unpublished Contemporaneous Account," *Science* 71 (14 March 1930), p. 286; *New York Evening Post*, 29 January 1812, 5 February 1812; Flint, *Recollections*, p. 218; Henry McMurtrie, *Sketches of Louisville and Its Environs* (Louisville: S. Penn, 1819), p. 245; Daniel Drake, *Natural and Statistical View or Picture of Cincinnati and the Miami Country* (Cincinnati: Looker and Wallace, 1815), p. 235; John Haywood, *The Natural and Aboriginal History of Tennessee* (Nashville: George Wilson, 1823), pp. 32–33; St. Louis *Louisiana Gazette*, 22 February 1812; Philadelphia *Pennsylvania Gazette*, 29 January 1812; Audubon, *Audubon and His Journals*, pp. 234–35.

separately, and distinctly upon the ear, not breaking upon or being lost or confused in each other.[9]

After the terrible shocks of 7 February, disturbing reports from the afflicted zone briefly caused the flow of commerce to be reduced to a trickle. A great deal of property in the form of boats and cargoes had been destroyed or abandoned. What escaped destruction was often "disposed of by their affrighted owners for a trifle." Mathias Speed, who reached New Madrid on 7 February, began walking north five days later. The report he wrote for the *Bardstown Repository* on 3 March was anything but encouraging: "From what I had seen and heard I was deterred from proceeding further, and nearly gave away what property I had." A few hardy souls made the effort in March. James McBride purchased two flatboats on the Miami and embarked with a load of flour, whiskey, and pork. He intended to sell his cargo in New Orleans, go around by sea to Philadelphia, and purchase more goods to haul back to Ohio. This was a common enough circle for the river commerce of the day, but "the reports prevailing of the dangers to be encountered from the Indians and the Earthquakes had so much frightened the people that none would venture to encounter them." The lure of higher profits was enough to motivate men of McBride's kidney, and news of their success quickly restored commerce on the river to its normal flow.[10]

It took weeks and often months for mail to reach the east coast from the Mississippi Valley, and rumors

9. McMurtrie, *Sketches of Louisville,* p. 245.

10. Letter from "A Citizen of Kentucky," *Bardstown Repository* (n.d.), in National Archives, Record Group 59, Department of State, vol. 1, "Territorial Papers, Minnesota– Missouri," p. 32; Flint, *Recollections,* p. 219; Philadelphia *Pennsylvania Gazette,* 18 March 1812; James McBride, "Brief Accounts of Journies in the Western Country, 1809– 1812," *Quarterly Publication of the Historical and Philosophical Society of Ohio* 5:1 (January– March 1910):27– 28.

sprouted riotously as a result. As late as 31 January the *New York Evening Post* printed a report from Charleston, South Carolina, that Natchez had sunk and 4,000 persons had perished.[11] Both the size of Natchez and its extinction were exaggerated. Gradually it became clear that there were remarkably few casualties. The vicious quake in Venezuela in March extinguished the lives of thousands of people. But the New Madrid earthquakes, much longer in duration and involving many shocks as powerful as the fatal one in Venezuela, took comparatively few lives.

The exact number of deaths will never be known. The two women at New Madrid, the Negro drowned in a sinkhole, and the six Indians killed in the vicinity by caving banks have been mentioned. A man was drowned near the White River in Arkansas by a sudden rise in the water on 16 December, and a young boy, searching for missing cattle in the St. Francis swamps, disappeared.[12] Beyond these, as far as deaths on land are concerned, the record is silent.

The record on the river was vaguer but altogether suggestive of greater carnage. Most accounts dealt with lost boats but were often silent on the fate of the crew. Some narrators remarked on the caving of the banks, which crushed boats and men. "Many boats were overwhelmed in this manner, and their crews perished." The tidal-wave effect caused by the falling banks swamped boats on the river beyond reach of land. One report mentioned a flatboat lost in this way, its six-man crew drowned. Many more must have suffered the same fate.

11. *New York Evening Post,* 31 January 1812.

12. St. Louis *Louisiana Gazette,* 22 February 1812; *Pittsburgh Gazette,* 14 February 1812; Timothy Dudley, "The Earthquake of 1811 at New Madrid, Missouri (from the Narrative of an Eyewitness)," *Annual Report of the Board of Regents of the Smithsonian Institution . . . for the Year 1858* (Washington: William A. Harris, Printer, 1859), p. 422.

Some reports were specific, giving the exact number of boats lost that had been observed locally. Others said simply, "several lives were lost among the boatmen."[13] Generally, the evidence was indirect even from firsthand observers.

Whilst we were waiting till the light became sufficient for us to embark, two canoes floated down the river, in one of which we saw some Indian corn and some clothes. We considered this as a melancholy proof that some of the boats we passed the preceding day had perished. Our conjectures were afterwards confirmed, as we learned that three had been overwhelmed, and that all on board had perished.[14]

It is noteworthy that most of the deaths reported on land were from drowning. High fatalities would normally be the result of falling structures, but there are no reports of a building collapsing on the occupants within. The low density of the population near the quake's center must be kept in mind. Narrow streets teeming with panicky crowds, a death trap in so many historic earthquakes, were absent from the scene, as was the aftermath of fire so devastating at San Francisco in 1906. The villages of New Madrid and Little Prairie had only a few hundred residents living in widely spaced houses. The majority of the people of the region were scattered on farms in the hinterland. Both towns were far enough from the epicenter to escape total devastation in the first series of shocks. The destruction of Little Prairie on 16 December was mainly the result of flooding. New Madrid's houses remained intact. On the whole the later shocks were more damaging to houses than the earlier ones, partly because structures had

13. Hildreth, "History of a Voyage," p. 130; James T. Lloyd, *Lloyd's Steamboat Directory and Disasters on the Western Waters* (Cincinnati: J. T. Lloyd and Co., 1856), p. 320; *Pittsburgh Gazette,* 13 March 1812; *New York Evening Post,* 11 February 1812; Mitchill. "Detailed Narrative," pp. 300–301.

14. *Bradbury's Travels,* p. 206.

been weakened but also because the epicenters moved on a northeasterly line closer to both sites in the later series.

The absence of fatalities from collapsing houses has generally been attributed to the prevalence of the characteristic log cabin, which was considered to be more elastic than a brick or masonry structure.[15] Many of the houses at New Madrid were frame, however. These withstood the early shocks, and when they finally collapsed no one was living in them; the people had retreated to temporary camps. Unfortunately, the experience of New Madrid and Little Prairie showed that nothing would stand near the epicenter. Nothing was standing at Little Prairie in March, and according to one account of New Madrid "the houses of brick, stone and log are torn to pieces, and those of frame thrown upon their sides."[16] The shocks of 7 February, when the epicenter was closer, had brought everything down. Nevertheless, the relative advantages of timber over brick emerge clearly from the earthquake narratives. Brick chimneys were the first to go at New Madrid, and chimneys were toppled over an area of many hundreds of miles. At places as widely distributed as St. Louis, Natchez, and Savannah, brick and stone buildings were cracked. Given the general character of the lower Mississippi Valley as a major earthquake zone, the lesson would seem to have been clear; but it went unheeded. Timber structures "are disappearing in all directions," Flint said of the region in 1832. "Brick and stone houses have been generally preferred."[17]

15. Nathaniel Southgate Shaler, "Earthquakes of the Western United States," *Atlantic Monthly* 24:145 (November 1869):554–55; Murat Halstead, *The World on Fire* (New York: International Publishing Co., 1902), p. 121.

16. *New York Evening Post,* 11 March 1812; McBride, "Brief Accounts," p. 29.

17. Timothy Flint, *The History and Geography of the Mississippi*

The New Madrid Earthquakes

The sounds, sights, and smells of the earthquakes contributed to the terror. The sounds in particular were so varied they were difficult to distinguish. The cracking and crashing of trees, the cries of wildfowl, the rush of wind where there was no wind, explosions, an ominous subterranean rumble, a roaring, rushing, hissing, or whistling noise were all variously reported. Fuller said "the sound in the Mississippi Valley was a somewhat dull roar, rather than the rumbling sound of thunder with which it was compared at certain of the remote localities"; but both kinds of sound were reported within the zone of principal disturbance as well as at varying distances from it. Distance did make a difference in the quality and intensity of sound. Daniel Drake reported that the noise at Cincinnati "was a peculiar, faint, dull rumbling or rushing sound," but "the principal shocks on the Mississippi, were attended or preceded by an explosive sound; which the people of that region denominate subterranean thunder."[18]

In their descriptions, many people attempted to translate the unknown and unexpected into comfortable and recognizable figures of speech. Thirteen different narrators described the sound preceding the

<hr>

Valley, vol. 1 (Cincinnati: E. H. Flint and L. R. Lincoln, 1832), p. 296. This is not the place for an inventory of every toppled chimney, but those interested in the effects of the earthquakes on brick and masonry over a widely distributed area might begin with the following sources: St. Louis *Louisiana Gazette,* 21 December 1811, 28 December 1811; *New York Evening Post,* 31 January 1812, 5 March 1812; Drake, *Natural and Statistical View,* pp. 26– 27; McMurtrie, *Sketches of Louisville,* p. 233; Adam Walker, *A Journal of Two Campaigns of the Fourth Regiment of U.S. Infantry* (Keene, N. H.: Printed by the author, 1816), pp. 38– 39; Myron L. Fuller, "The New Madrid Earthquake," U.S. Geological Survey *Bulletin* 494 (Washington: Government Printing Office, 1912), *passim,* has much information on the subject.

18. Fuller, "New Madrid Earthquake," p. 102; Drake, *Natural and Statistical View,* pp. 235, 238.

shocks as the distant rumble of thunder, often underground. Seven compared it to carriages "passing over a paved road," and six thought it sounded like "the reports of heavy artillery." These descriptions came from points distant from one another, from Charleston, South Carolina; Savannah, Georgia; and Annapolis, Maryland; as well as from Natchez and New Madrid, and they very likely refer to the same sound—indeed, two of the narratives contain both the thunder and cannon analogies. Three witnesses, all from the Ohio or Mississippi valleys, spoke of a roaring noise accompanied, according to two of them, by hissing or whistling. Three others added further to the metaphorical confusion by speaking of "a blowing noise, resembling that made by a smith's bellows."[19]

There may have been a ubiquitous sound heard as the waves passing through the ground were refracted into the atmosphere and described variously by individual observers. But some sounds clearly had local causes. A sand blow erupted with a loud explosion, but a "roaring

19. R. A. Campbell, ed., *Campbell's Gazetteer of Missouri* (St. Louis: R. A. Campbell 1874), p. 394; Drake, *Natural and Statistical View,* p. 238; Winthrop Sargent, "Account of Several Shocks of an Earthquake in the Southern and Western Parts of the United States," *Memoirs of the American Academy of Arts and Sciences* 3:2 (1815):352, 355; Dow, *History of Cosmopolite,* p. 344; Pusey, "New Madrid Earthquake," pp. 285–86; McBride, "Brief Accounts," p. 30; St. Louis *Louisiana Gazette,* 21 December 1811, 22 February 1812; Philadelphia *Pennsylvania Gazette,* 1 January 1812, 12 February 1812, 18 March 1812, 6 May 1812; *Pittsburgh Gazette,* 31 January 1812, 14 February 1812; *New York Evening Post,* 26 December 1811, 1 January 1812, 29 January 1812, 5 March 1812; Mitchill, "Detailed Narrative," pp. 285–86; Fuller, "New Madrid Earthquake," p. 22; Lloyd, *Lloyd's Steamboat Directory,* pp. 320–21; Alphonso Wetmore, *Gazetteer of the State of Missouri* (St. Louis: C. Keemle, 1837), p. 139; Nolte, *Fifty Years in Both Hemispheres,* p. 182; Hildreth, "History of a Voyage," p. 129; Bringier, "Notices of the Geology," pp. 20–21; Haywood, *Natural and Statistical History,* p. 32.

and whistling" sound accompanied the ejection of sand. The very stones found voice in some locations, their rattle making a noise "similar to that of the wheels of a wagon in a pebbly road." Some sources mentioned the sound of wind as loud as a tempest even though the air was still, which may have been caused by the shaking of the trees. Pierce said the "forest shook like rushes," producing a sound like "a severe wind passing through a large cane brake."[20] The falling of the banks along the river no doubt contributed to the cacophony. Indeed, this was not strictly an earthquake phenomenon but one rivermen were quite accustomed to, although banks fell in unprecedented number during the shocks. Ever shifting and changing, the mighty river nibbled incessantly at its soft alluvial banks, and descriptions of their collapse were often reminiscent of the earthquake narratives. "The traveller . . . frequently sees huge masses of earth fall . . . into the bed of the river. These masses sometimes constitute an acre and are covered with a heavy growth of trees. The noise, occasioned by the falling of the banks, is as loud as distant thunder but far more impressive."[21]

There were as many descriptions of "flashes of light" or a red glow in the sky as there were references to sound, and these were spread over just as wide an area.[22] In some instances there were probably electrical storms in the vicinity, as Fuller suggested. But Decem-

20. *New York Evening Post,* 11 February 1812; Bringier, "Notices of the Geology," pp. 20–21; Haywood, *Natural and Aboriginal History,* p. 31.

21. Estwick Evans, *A Pedestrious Tour* (Concord, N.H.: Joseph C. Spear, 1819), p. 196.

22. See, for instance, Haywood, *Natural and Aboriginal History,* p. 33; Mitchill, "Detailed Narrative," pp. 299–300; Drake, *Natural and Statistical View,* p. 235; Flint, *Recollections,* p. 217; Philadelphia *Pennsylvania Gazette,* 29 January 1812; *New York Evening Post,* 22 February 1812.

ber was an unusual time for such storms to occur, and the number of the reports as well as their wide distribution argued for some other cause related to the earthquakes.[23] Some people regarded the lights as confirmation of the belief that earthquakes were caused by electrical fluid.[24]

A symphony of horrid sounds and flashes of light were accompanied by a pervasive odor. Fuller attributed this to the widespread ejection of buried organic matter in the area of principal disturbance but thought the odors "represented normal atmospheric condensations which happened to be coincident with the earthquake disturbance" at more remote localities. If so, the coincidence was remarkable. At Columbia, South Carolina; Savannah, Georgia; New Madrid; at points on the Mississippi; and at many other places the odor was described almost always as sulphurous.[25] For the people of the time the smell of brimstone was unnecessary confirmation that their surroundings had been suddenly transformed into a hell.

Thoughts of perdition and the landslides of the earthquakes brought many backsliding Christians up

23. Fuller, "New Madrid Earthquake," p. 47.

24. There were also reports by Bryan, Lesieur, and others of a sudden darkness of the atmosphere that descended in the wake of the hard shocks. The cause was identified by the author of the "New Madrid Extract" as dust.

25. Fuller, "New Madrid Earthquake," p. 46; Haywood, *Natural and Aboriginal History,* p. 31; Mitchill, "Detailed Narrative," pp. 284, 293; St. Louis *Louisiana Gazette,* 22 February 1812; *Pittsburgh Gazette,* 31 January 1812; New Orleans *Louisiana Gazette and Daily Advertiser,* 20 January 1812. C. F. Volney, *A View of the Soil and Climate of the United States of America* (Philadelphia: J. Conrad and Co., 1804), pp. 97–98, quoted an authority who asserted that "the fetid smell of liver of sulphur" accompanied the earthquakes that occurred in eastern North America between 1628 and 1782. See also Lesieur to A. D. Hager, 28 June 1871, in which he admits that the odor may have been petroleum, an odor not generally familiar to people at the time of the earthquakes, perhaps associated with

short. After the first shock at New Madrid people of all faiths gathered outdoors and offered thanks for their deliverance. The same scene was repeated after the evacuation of 7 February. Flint added a characteristic touch of pathos: "The cattle, as much terrified as the rational creation, crowded about the assemblage of men." If there was no preacher, as was usually the case, people in the smaller Mississippi River settlements gathered around a Bible and someone capable of reading it.[26]

Quick to take advantage of this awesome manifestation of Divine Power, preachers flocked to the afflicted region. In western Kentucky James Finley leaped upon a table after a tremor had begun and shouted: "For the great day of his wrath is come, and who shall be able to stand?" That night, he said with pardonable modesty, "would never be forgotten in time or eternity." Many hardened sinners fell "like those slain in battle." During the shocks grown men were known to fall to the floor groaning and pass out from terror. Finley was in Ohio, near Zanesville, during a daylight shock on 16 December. "Consternation sat on every countenance, especially upon the wicked," he observed with relish. They "fled into the streets, clinging one to another, and crying for mercy." When a shock had passed, people raised their voices in "grateful thanks to the Supreme Ruler of

asphaltum, which Hager, a scientist, thought may have been the "species of charcoal" described by Lesieur and others as ejected from sand blows; in Daughters of the American Revolution, Lucy Jefferson Lewis Chapter (New Madrid), "New Madrid Earthquakes, 1811–12, compiled from the New Madrid archive in New Madrid county courthouse," manuscript in the Missouri Historical Society Library, St. Louis, Mo.

26. John Wells Foster, *The Mississippi Valley: Its Physical Geography* (Chicago: S. C. Griggs and Co., 1869), p. 20; John Shaw, "New Madrid Earthquake: Account of Colonel John Shaw," *Missouri Historical Review* 6 (January 1912): 91; Flint, *Recollections,* p. 217; *Bradbury's Travels,* p. 209.

Nature" for their preservation. But the return of the shocks, even during a sermon, sent them shrieking and running for the outdoors. "It was a time of great terror to sinners."[27]

For ten years the western settlements had been the scenes of appalling outbursts of religious enthusiasm, but on the whole the Devil had held up his end. The majority of the settlers were unchurched. Louisville had a theater before the first house of God was built, and, according to one account, it was the earthquakes that reminded citizens of the omission.[28] The churches had grown impressively and steadily for ten years, but in 1812 a great harvest was gathered. The earthquakes

contributed greatly to increase the interest on the subject of religion. Multitudes who previously paid no attention to the subject of religion, now flocked out to meeting, and the power of God was manifested, not only in the earthquake and the fire, but in the still small yet powerful voice. The number of converts was great, and the work extended almost everywhere.[29]

In the whole of Tennessee, Kentucky, and portions of Mississippi, Arkansas, Illinois, Indiana, Ohio, and western Virginia, where the earthquakes were felt forcefully, the largest of the sects, the Methodist church, increased its membership from 30,741 in 1811 to 45,983 in 1812. This was a gain of 50 per cent during a time when the number of Methodists in the rest of the

27. W. P. Strickland, ed., *Autobiography of Rev. James B. Finley; or, Pioneer Life in the West* (Cincinnati: Methodist Book Concern, 1854), pp. 238–40; Walter Brownlow Posey, "The Earthquake of 1811 and Its Influence on Evangelistic Methods in the Churches of the Old South," *Tennessee Historical Magazine* 1:2 (1931): 110; Philadelphia *Pennsylvania Gazette,* 5 February 1812.

28. Benjamin Casseday, *The History of Louisville from Its Earliest Settlement till the Year 1852* (Louisville: Hull and Brothers, 1852), pp. 125–26.

29. Strickland, *Autobiography of James B. Finley,* pp. 238–40.

nation increased by less than 1 per cent. There was a relative decline in the next couple of years before the steady upward climb resumed, indicating a degree of backsliding as the unregenerate realized the world's end was not forthcoming. "Earth-quake Christian" was a phrase embittered preachers reserved for those whose devotions were more enthusiastic during the course of the shocks than before and after.

The record number of conversions was a symptom of a preoccupation with eschatology characteristic of the times. Simple people looked on the wars and rumors of wars, natural disasters, and signs in the heavens as portents, but even educated men found it difficult to ignore the manifestations—to wonder, in short, if someone were trying to tell them something. As a result, many fearful people flocked to the Church for refuge.[30]

Not the least among the numerous signs was the appearance of the comet. It was seen around the world at different times over the course of the year. Sighted in France in March and visible there for three months, observations were also made at the Cape of Good Hope and other points south of the equator. It was generally visible in the United States from 6 September until 16 January. "Peculiarly brilliant," often described as beautiful, it shed a "twilight over the forests" of the west whenever the generally cloudy conditions of December abated, suffusing the night with a glow resembling "the light of an aurora borealis." The impression it made varied with the sophistication of the observer. In Boston a small literary journal named *The Comet* began publishing in October, announcing that it "expected a

30. Posey, "The Earthquake and the Churches," pp. 111–13; Shaw, "New Madrid Earthquake," p. 92; Wayne Viitanen, "The Winter the Mississippi Ran Backwards," p. 66; Mitchill, "Detailed Narrative," pp. 281–82; Drake, *Natural and Statistical View,* pp. 239–40.

train of light" to follow it. But the last number in January rather fulfilled another prediction, that it would "soon *pass off into the regions of space* and become *invisible.*" Given the coincidence of its appearance, it was inevitable that the comet would be associated with the earthquakes. A writer for one newspaper wondered with nervous jocularity if it had "touched the mountain of *California,* that has given a small shake to this side of the globe."[31]

Less sophisticated people were not inclined to be jocose. Instead, they reacted with nervous apprehension. Comets had always been considered harbingers of disaster. It was probably this same one that Leo Tolstoy used in *War and Peace* to presage Napoleon's invasion of Russia, and it mingled with the eschatology of the earthquakes. "The tail of the comet was bifurcated," according to the scientist Nathaniel Bowditch, "and near the middle part of the space between the two forked points the colour was as dark as the unilluminated part of the heavens." On his journey downriver John Bradbury paused at a small settlement near the

31. Nathaniel Bowditch, "Elements of the Orbit of the Comet of 1811," *Memoirs of the American Academy of Arts and Sciences* 3 (1815): 313; Winthrop Sargent, "Account of Several Shocks of an Earthquake," p. 357; Mitchill, "Detailed Narrative," pp. 285–86; Charles Joseph Latrobe, *The Rambler in North America,* vol. 1 (London: R. B. Seeley and W. Burnside, 1835), pp. 102–3; John Farrar, "Observations of the Comet of 1811," *Memoirs of the American Academy of Arts and Sciences* 3 (1815): 308; *The Comet* 1–13 (19 October 1811–11 January 1812), quotes from issue of 19 October; New Orleans *Louisiana Gazette and Daily Advertiser,* 21 December 1811. William Leigh Pierce made the connection in verse:

Nature convulsed!—with terrors shook the earth,
And omens usher'd in the monstrous birth!—
Along the blue expanse with flaming locks
The comet blazes, while creation rocks.

Pierce, *The Year: A Poem in Three Cantoes* (New York: David Longworth, 1813), p. 23.

fourth Chickasaw Bluff, where he found terrified squatters gathered around a local savant who explained that the earth had rolled over one of the "two horns" of the comet and was trapped between them. The shocks were caused by the efforts of the earth to extricate itself. "If this should be accomplished, all would be well, if otherwise, inevitable destruction to the world would follow." The enlightened Bradbury was disposed to be amused, and others also made light of the doomsday theme: "*Sodom and Gomorrha* would have been saved had three righteous persons been found in it—we therefore hope that Natchez has been saved on the same principle." For others the "immediate dissolution of the world!" was a matter to be taken seriously. "Glory, glory, glory to God!" shouted a woman in Putnam, Ohio, as she ran into the streets, clapping her hands during the shocks of 16 December. "My savior is coming! I am my Lord's and he is mine!" Others were less confident, like the wretch who remembered suddenly that "he had been a very bad man."[32]

Few records were kept of the effects of the earthquakes upon the Indian nations. One of the few references to the western range of the earthquakes was an indication that they were felt by the Otoes, who lived on the Missouri River near the present Kansas-Nebraska border. The earthquakes had an obvious effect on many tribes and created an eschatological response similar to that of the settlers. A white captive living with the Osage tribe left a rare description of Indian reaction: The "Indians were filled with great terror, on account of the repeated occurrences of vio-

32. Bowditch, "Elements of the Orbit of the Comet of 1811," p. 324; *Bradbury's Travels,* p. 209; New Orleans *Louisiana Gazette and Daily Advertiser,* 21 December 1811; Strickland, *Autobiography of James B. Finley,* pp. 238–40; Posey, "The Earthquake and the Churches," p. 110.

lent tremors and oscillations of the earth; the trees and wigwams shook exceedingly; the ice which skirted the margin of the Arkansas river was broken in pieces; and most of the Indians thought that the Great Spirit, angry with the human race, was about to destroy the world."[33]

Indians outnumbered the settlers in the zone of principal disturbance. Spanish policy had deliberately encouraged immigration of white and red from American territories, and a considerable population of Delawares, Shawnees, and Cherokees were scattered in villages along the St. Francis and White rivers. Outlawed or ostracized groups from the Creek, Chocktaw, and Chickasaw nations were also settled in the region. The earthquake narratives often used Indian towns as points of reference for locating and describing damage to fords and other strategic geographic points. On the whole, these records contain nothing of the towns themselves, although many were located in the eye of the convulsion and must have suffered greatly. The scanty references were tantalizing: "Certain Indians had arrived near the mouth of the [Arkansas] river, who had seen a large lake or sea, where many of their brothers had resided, and had perished." There were also references to parties of Indians that were scouring the country for persons missing as a result of the disasters, and others to religious ceremonies held to propitiate the mighty forces unleashed by the earthquakes. Certainly, the death toll would have been higher had Indian casualties been counted. On the eastern side of the Mississippi was the territory of the Chickasaw Nation. According to an Indian legend Reelfoot Lake was named after a

33. Edwin James, *Account of an Expedition from Pittsburgh to the Rocky Mountains,* vol. 65 (Ann Arbor: University Microfilms, 1966), p. 272; *Pittsburgh Gazette,* 7 February 1812; John Dunn Hunter, *Memoirs of a Captivity Among the Indians of North America,* edited by Richard Drinnon (New York: Schocken Books, 1973), p. 25.

chief, so called because of his clubfoot and lumbering gait, who stole a princess from the Chocktaws to take as a wife, despite a warning in a dream that if he did so the earth would tremble in rage. During the wedding ceremony the ground shook, the townsite sank, and the Mississippi gathered its waters and flowed backward over it, drowning everyone.[34]

The sun had almost set for the native peoples of the Ohio country. They had struggled valiantly, but their bravest warriors were slain, and the future offered a bleak choice between extermination and removal beyond the Mississippi. A brooding misery had settled upon the tribes in the years before the earthquakes. Yet beneath the surface vague, often shapeless movement could be detected. Never united, long dependent on white technology and trade goods, the Indians were implicated in their own downfall. The dawning awareness of this fact might have produced, in time, a genuine cultural and political nationalism. Time had run out, but there were indications that this "rough beast" was slouching "towards Bethlehem to be born."

Many Indians believed that they had betrayed the old

34. Amos Stoddard, *Sketches, Historical and Descriptive, of Louisiana* (Philadelphia: Mathew Carey, 1812), p. 210; Clarence Edwin Carter, ed., *Territorial Papers of the United States,* vol. 14; *Louisiana–Missouri, 1806–1814* (Washington: Government Printing Office, 1949), p. 624; Philadelphia *Pennsylvania Gazette,* 11 March 1812, 18 March 1812; St. Louis *Louisiana Gazette,* 21 March 1812; Federal Writer's Project, *Tennessee: A Guide to the State* (New York: Viking Press, 1939), p. 429; George R. Mayfield, "Reelfoot Lake, the Problem Child of Tennessee," *Tennessee Academy of Science Journal* 25 (April 1950): 149. Whites also had tall tales concerning the lake's origin. Through an oversight, according to one wag, the Lord forgot about the lake during the original creation. "When he finally did remember it, after goodness knows how many thousand years, he was so put out about it he didn't think about it bein' Sunday, and he jest ripped up the earth and made that lake as quick as he could." Wayne Viitanen, "Folklore and Fakelore of an Earthquake," *Kentucky Folklore Record* 19 (1973): 106.

ways of their fathers. Convulsive attempts to achieve purification sometimes afflicted entire villages in a consuming fury. The Delawares and Shawnees on the St. Francis River experienced such an outbreak. Numerous victims were executed by fire for obscure reasons in a frenzy that puzzled white observers, and the burnings only ceased, so the account went, with the arrival of Tecumseh,[35] an individual who had the qualities needed to give direction to formless yearning. This Shawnee chief was the equal in nobility and inherent ability of the greatest statesmen of the age. He ranged over astonishing distances conveying a message with all the force and eloquence at his command: Only national and cultural unity among the tribes could prevent further white encroachments. His brother, Tenskwatawa, called the Prophet, was a religious leader and mystic who called for Indian spiritual regeneration. His converts flocked to Tippecanoe on the Wabash and became recruits for Tecumseh. Thus the movement they headed had a religious-cultural as well as political-military dimension. The military power of this movement was broken in November by the army of William Henry Harrison, and it never recovered from the blow.[36]

Tecumseh was absent from the battle of Tippecanoe. He had gone into the south to carry his message to the Chocktaw, Chickasaw, Creek, Seminole, and Cherokee. Through the fall and early winter he continued his travels, unaware of the defeat of his hopes. He had indifferent success, although a faction of the Creeks did eventually take the warpath, called by the name of the "Red Sticks" Tecumseh had distributed among them. One legend has it that William Weatherford, the half-

35. Campbell, *Campbell's Gazetteer of Missouri*, p. 394.
36. Glenn Tucker, *Tecumseh: Vision of Glory* (New York: Bobbs-Merrill Co., 1956), *passim*.

Scot war chief, was finally converted when Tecumseh accurately forecasted the earthquakes. The incident took place at an ancient Creek town near the site of Montgomery, Alabama.

He made his way to the lodge of the chief called the Big Warrior. He explained his object, delivered his war talk, presented a bundle of sticks, gave a piece of wampum and a war hatchet—all which the Big Warrior took—when Tecumthé, reading the spirit and intentions of the Big Warrior, looked him in the eye, and, pointing his finger toward his face, said: "Your blood is white. You have taken my talk, and the sticks, and the wampum, and the hatchet, but you do not mean to fight. I know the reason. You do not believe the Great Spirit has sent me. You shall know. I leave Tuckhabatchee directly, and shall go straight to Detroit. When I arrive there, I will stamp on the ground with my foot and shake down every house in Tuckhabatchee." So saying, he turned and left the Big Warrior in utter amazement at both his manner and his threat, and pursued his journey. The Indians were struck no less with his conduct than was the Big Warrior, and began to dread the arrival of the day when the threatened calamity would befall them. They met often and talked over this matter, and counted the days carefully to know the day when Tecumthé would reach Detroit. The morning they had fixed upon as the day of his arrival at last came. A mighty rumbling was heard—the Indians all ran out of their houses—the earth began to shake; when at last, sure enough, every house in Tuckhabatchee was shaken down. The exclamation was in every mouth, "Tecumthé has got to Detroit!" The effect was electric. The message he had delivered to the Big Warrior was believed, and many of the Indians took their rifles and prepared for the war. The reader will not be surprised to learn that an earthquake had produced all this; but he will be doubtless, that it should happen on the very day on which Tecumthé arrived at Detroit, and in exact fulfillment of his threat. It was the famous earthquake of New Madrid on the Mississippi.[37]

---

37. Quoted in James Mooney, "The Ghost-Dance Religion and the Sioux Outbreak of 1890," *Fourteenth Annual Report of the Bureau of American Ethnology for 1892–93* 14:2 (Washington: Government

Effects and Responses

While the fact of the prediction may be doubted, the existence of the legend was evidence of an Indian response analogous to that of the settlers. Tecumseh clearly recognized the potential usefulness of the earthquakes for his purposes. A white captive, John Dunn Hunter, recalled the chief's speech as he moved among the Osage in Missouri on his return trip from the south early in 1812, still ignorant of Tippecanoe. *"Brothers*—The Great Spirit is angry with our enemies; he speaks in thunder, and the earth swallows up villages, and drinks up the Mississippi. The great waters will cover their lowlands; their corn cannot grow; and the Great Spirit will sweep those who escape to the hills from the earth with his terrible breath."[38]

These words reached forward in time, expressing an "eschatological vision," in the words of Hunter's able editor Richard Drinnon, that "was a direct anticipation of the Ghost Dance religion decades later."[39] The anthropologist James Mooney demonstrated long ago that the Ghost Dance doctrine of Wovoka and Sitting Bull that broke out among the Sioux in 1890 was "only the latest of a series of Indian religious revivals," reaching back more than a century.

When the race lies crushed and groaning beneath an alien yoke, how natural is the dream of a redeemer, an Arthur, who shall return from exile or awake from some long sleep to

---

Printing Office, 1896): 687. Mooney was relying on Thomas L. McKenney and James Hall, *History of the Indian Tribes of America,* 3 vols. (Philadelphia: F. W. Greenough, 1838–1844). Relying on a different source, Tucker, *Tecumseh,* p. 211, quotes the Indian leader as saying that the earthquake would occur when he got back to Tippecanoe. However, Tecumseh was in neither place when the earthquakes began. Both accounts apparently came out of an oral tradition among the Creeks. It was Tucker who said that Weatherford began to prepare for war after the earthquake.

38. Hunter, *Memoirs of a Captivity Among the Indians,* p. 31.
39. Ibid., p. 235.

drive out the usurper and win back for his people what they have lost. The hope becomes a faith and the faith becomes the creed of priests and prophets, until the hero is a god and the dream a religion, looking to some great miracle of nature for its culmination and accomplishment. The doctrines of the Hindu avatar, the Hebrew Messiah, the Christian millennium, and the Hesûnanin of the Indian Ghost Dance are essentially the same, and have their origin in a hope and longing common to all humanity.[40]

The Day of Judgment, made so immediate for many whites by the earthquakes, had its counterpart among Indians who shared in the great religious revival of their time. For Tecumseh, a genuine Arthurian figure in this catastrophic tradition, the earthquakes were a signal that the Great Spirit had finally taken a decisive hand in the affairs of his people. The Indian Armageddon was at hand.

Among whites the theme of retribution for usurpers was present also. After the shocks of December the inhabitants of New Madrid were told by an Indian in the vicinity that the Prophet had "caused the earthquake to destroy the whites." On the river many boatmen thought the first shock was a result of Indian "mischief."[41] Retribution for the usurper was the theme of *Transallegania; or, the Groans of Missouri,* a wretched epic poem by Henry Rowe Schoolcraft. A glassmaker from western New York whose career as a manufacturer was ended abruptly after the Treaty of Ghent (1815) by the competition of foreign glass, Schoolcraft went west to seek his fortune.[42] In 1818 he visited

40. Monney, "Ghost-Dance Religion," pp. 654, 657.

41. Philadelphia *Pennsylvania Gazette,* 12 February 1812; *New York Evening Post,* 11 February 1812; James H. Perkins, *Annals of the West* (Cincinnati: J. R. Albach, 1846), p. 520; Hildreth, "History of a Voyage," pp. 129–30.

42. Chase S. Osborn and Stellanova Osborn, *Schoolcraft, Longfellow, Hiawatha* (Lancaster, Pa.: Jaques Cattell Press, 1942), pp. 308–45.

Missouri and the Ozarks, and the result was a poem that remains today the only serious attempt in American literature to make use of the earthquakes. In this fanciful account the vast tide of immigration to the west aroused the ire of the King of the Metals, who called all of his subjects, the ores and minerals of the earth, to a council in a subterranean chamber to consult on a course of action. The debate became noisy and heated.

And such heats were begat among metals and stones,
That the cave filled with sulphur, and bellowed with groans;
And the earth, as if grasped by omnipotent might,
Quaked dreadful, and shook with the throes of affright;
Deep northwardly rolled the electrical jar,
Creating amazement, destruction, and war;
The rivers they boiled like a pot over coals,
And mortals fell prostrate, and prayed for their souls:
Every rock on our borders cracked, quivered, and shrunk,
And Nackitosh tumbled, and New Madrid sunk.[43]

Schoolcraft himself was never brought to justice. Indeed, he went on to become a leading American authority on Indians; but the poem sank, like New Madrid, into quiet obscurity.

43. In Louisiana both the French and English pronunciation of Nachitoches was and remains today "Nackitosh"—but Nachitoches did not tumble. H. R. Schoolcraft, *Transallegania; or, the Groans of Missouri* (New York: J. Seymour, Printer, 1820), p. 23.

6. A Question of Causation

As the mass of the people are seldom able to rise to general views, and are consequently always disposed to ascribe great phenomena to local telluric and atmospheric processes, wherever the shaking of the earth is continued for a long time, fears of the eruption of a new volcano are awakened.

Alexander von Humboldt (1849)

When such earthquakes of the size of the 1811– 1812 sequence recur, the emotional problems which will result for large numbers of people in the widely affected area will likely be severe.

Otto W. Nuttli (1973)

People ascribed the earthquakes to a variety of causes. A few may have accused themselves, such as the gentleman who worried about the copper he had buried as a part of the process for manufacturing counterfeit money, anxious that perhaps an unexpected and unhealthy chemical reaction had occurred. Others looked to the heavens and eyed the comet with suspicion or wondered if the earth and moon had come into contact. The territorial assembly of Missouri placed the blame squarely on the Divine Mechanic: "In the Catalogue of miseries and afflictions, with which it has pleased the Supreme being of the Universe, to visit the Inhabitants of this earth, there are none more truly awful and destructive than Earthquakes." Scientists were sometimes eager to assign the honor of an explanation to their own discipline. Thomas Nuttall, a botanist, believed that the shocks were caused by the decomposition of a "vast bed of lignite or wood-coal" under the surface: "How much has the vegetable kingdom to do with the destiny of man!" More cautious, Samuel Latham Mitchill listed a variety of possibilities, from which the curious were invited to choose. For William Leigh Pierce the *primum mobile* was steam.[1]

The reaction of the editor of the St. Louis *Louisiana Gazette* was by far the most common: "Expecting the earth to be relieved by a volcanic eruption, I went out of doors and looked for the dreadful phenomenon." The operation of internal fire, often revealed elsewhere by the eruption of volcanoes, was widely believed to play a role in causing earthquakes. One early nineteenth-century writer, noting that the earthquakes that afflicted New England and Canada from the earliest days of settlement occurred along a northwest to southeast bias running from Lake Ontario to the Atlantic, announced that Ontario was the crater of an extinct volcano, thereby proving the existence of subterranean fires—although at great depths, since the lake was very deep.[2]

---

1. Walter Brownlow Posey, "The Earthquake of 1811 and Its Influence on Evangelistic Methods in the Churches of the Old South," *Tennessee Historical Magazine* 1 (1931):109; Philadelphia *Pennsylvania Gazette*, 12 February 1812; Clarence Edwin Carter, ed., *Territorial Papers of the United States,* vol. 14: *Louisiana–Missouri, 1806–1814* (Washington: Government Printing Office, 1949), pp. 729–30; Thomas Nuttall, *A Journal of Travels into the Arkansa Territory,* vol. 63 (Ann Arbor: University Microfilms, 1966), p. 53; Samuel Latham Mitchill, "A Detailed Narrative of the Earthquakes," *Transactions of the Literary and Philosophical Society of New York* 1 (1814); William Leigh Pierce, *The Year: A Poem in Three Cantoes* (New York: David Longworth, 1813).

2. St. Louis *Louisiana Gazette,* 21 December 1811; C. F. Volney, *A View of the Soil and Climate of the United States of America* (Philadelphia: J. Conrad and Co., 1804), pp. 98–99.

The New Madrid Earthquakes

The Mississippi Overflowing Its Banks
Courtesy of the Illinois State Historical Library, Springfield, Ill.

The New Madrid Earthquakes

It was precisely this association that lent credibility to the spurious narrative of John Clarke Edwards. His account was in the form of a letter from Asheville, North Carolina, that was first published in the *Raleigh Star* on 19 December. Edwards obviously was an educated man, and his lurid account seemed entirely plausible. Many descriptions of phenomena were realistic: "A hollow rumbling noise," ending in a dreadful crash, "a strong sulphurous stench"; but "fulminating" mountains "with flashes of fire seen issuing from their sides" and the destruction of a well-known landmark called the Painted Rock, which was allegedly strewn across the road to Knoxville, seemed to speak of unusual severity. A second letter embellished the scene with a fearsome live volcano:

> In the night time, the ignited stones, cinders, &c. which are thrown two or three hundred feet in the air, present a grand appearance, and have a great resemblance to artificial fireworks, such as rockets &c. During the day a column of whitish smoke issues from the crater; at night it has a flame-like appearance, and where it has been driven with the wind, has withered the small dwarf pines which had taken root in the barren soil of this and the neighbouring mountains. Their bark and leaves are incrusted with a yellowish powder, which has an acrid taste, and a small sulphuric smell.

He promised to "take another view of this western Aetna" in a few days and report further. After the *National Intelligencer* revealed that the volcano, the fall of Painted Rock, and several other ingenious inventions were a hoax, however, Edwards subsided into quiescence.[3]

For some time people continued to believe that the source of the disturbance was a volcano, generally thought to be somewhere west of the Mississippi. Con-

3. Philadelphia *Pennsylvania Gazette,* 29 January 1812, 19 February 1812, 26 February 1812.

A Question of Causation

firming evidence for this theory remained vague. "On the margin of our rivers," one account stated, "pumice and other volcanic matter is found," and there were many reports of pumice stone of considerable size seen floating down the Missouri. A black scum resembling soot appeared on the surface of the Mississippi during the shocks and fed such rumors. Wandering Indians claimed to have discovered a volcano on the headwaters of the Arkansas River; Indians had long been the source of rumors of smoking mountains located somewhere in the west.[4]

A widely accepted physical theory of the time held that the true origin of both volcanoes and earthquakes was the electric fluid. Earthquakes were known to travel very fast; one writer estimated that the shock of 1755 had spread over an area of four million square miles in a little over an hour. The cause of this speed was traced to electricity. There was one blind prediction that the earthquakes would be found to have originated in the Cordillera de Los Andes; the electrical "impulse which may be given by a volcano of the Andes would reach us in the course of an hour, or sooner, in proportion to the quantity of electric fluid affected by the contact." News of the destruction of Caracas made such conjectures seem almost prophetic.[5]

4. Ibid., 5 February 1812, 18 March 1812; St. Louis *Louisiana Gazette,* 29 February 1812; 21 December 1811; Amos Stoddard, *Sketches, Historical and Descriptive, of Louisiana* (Philadelphia: Mathew Carey, 1812), p. 241; Timothy Dudley, "The Earthquake of 1811 at New Madrid, Missouri (from the Narrative of an Eyewitness)," *Annual Report of the Board of Regents of the Smithsonian Institution . . . for the Year 1858* (Washington: William A. Harris, Printer, 1859), p. 423; Volney, *View of the Soil and Climate,* p. 101.

5. St. Louis *Louisiana Gazette,* 22 February 1812; Philadelphia *Pennsylvania Gazette,* 6 May 1812; Louis Bringier, "Notices of the Geology, Mineralogy, Topography, Production, and Aboriginal Inhabitants of the Regions around the Mississippi and Its Confluent Waters," *American Journal of Science and Arts* 3 (1821):20; Mitchill,

The New Madrid Earthquakes

Earthquakes did not depend on volcanoes at all, and were known to occur independently; "that subtle fluid" was the efficient cause of both and just about everything else. From the mid-eighteenth century electricity had evolved from a frivolous curiosity into the greatest force in the cosmos. Comte Georges Louis Leclerc de Buffon regarded it as the cause of all volcanic eruptions; Jean Baptiste de Monet, Chevalier de Lamarck, believed it was the prime mover behind organic evolution; the founder of Methodism, John Wesley, called it "the soul of the universe." This fluid "everywhere" pervaded "the interior of the earth," in the words of the editor of the St. Louis *Louisiana Gazette.* His source was the third edition of *Encyclopaedia Britannica* (1797), the last printed in America before the earthquakes, which attributed everything that happened on heaven and earth to its presence. Not only did electricity account for all terrestrial phenomena such as rain, snow, hail, lightning, and winds, but through the power of the magnet it guided the planets on their course through the heavens. "Whether we look to the heaven above or to the earth beneath, we can scarce perceive any thing that is not acted upon, and in a manner perfectly subjected to the operations of this wonderful fluid."[6]

"Detailed Narrative," p. 236; Janet Somerville Sachs, "Some Aspects of the Early History of Seismology," *Earthquake Information Bulletin* 11 (March–April 1979): 58–63.

6. I. Bernard Cohen, ed., *Benjamin Franklin's Experiments* (Cambridge: Harvard University Press, 1941), pp. 166–67; Stephen F. Mason, *A History of the Sciences* (New York: Collier Books, 1962), p. 474; A. Wolf, *A History of Science, Technology, and Philosophy in the Eighteenth Century* (London: George Allen and Unwin Ltd., 1952), pp. 388–90; Philip C. Ritterbush, *Overtures to Biology; The Speculations of Eighteenth-Century Naturalists* (New Haven: Yale University Press, 1964), pp. 18, 21, 27–28; St. Louis *Louisiana Gazette,* 15 February 1812, 22 February 1812; *Encyclopaedia; or, a Dictionary of Arts, Sciences, and Miscellaneous Literature,* vol. 6 (Philadelphia: Thomas Dobson, Printer, 1798), pp. 287, 535–39.

A Question of Causation

Inevitably it was believed to be the cause of earth-quakes, and although there were a few doubters, especially after the investigations that surrounded the Italian shocks at Calabria in 1783, the electrical fluid theory still held the field in that useful compendium, the *Britannica*. In America, with a few eccentric exceptions such as Nuttall, almost everyone with any pretensions to education turned to the electric fluid for an ultimate explanation of the earthquakes. The theory, simply put, was this: The subtle fluid was everywhere in the earth, but in evenly balanced quantities, and there was balance also between the amount in the earth and in the atmosphere. It was kept from accumulating in the earth in unhealthy quantities by passing into the atmosphere as vapor, water being the most common conductor. If for some reason it was prevented from escaping in this way it would necessarily find another outlet. It might discharge itself through a volcano or leap into the nearest ocean. But if a surplus of fluid accumulated at any point, and none of these outlets were available to it, then the "most terrible consequences" ensued, and it flew "against every obstacle with inconceivable violence." It would break out through those places that offered the least resistance. Water would leap out of the wells; dry wells were long associated with the aftermath of earthquakes. Trees, houses, steeples, and other structures, because of their height relatively less oppressed by the weight of the atmosphere, would be suddenly and horribly transformed into escape hatches for the pent-up forces. Then, indeed, would the voice of Nature speak in thunder.[7]

Modern seismological theory is more complex, but only recently have answers to the questions of ultimate causation taken a form more sophisticated than such

7. *Encyclopaedia*, pp. 281–82.

universal explanations as the electric fluid. Partly this slowness was the result of the infant state of the science. Although its origins are in the eighteenth and nineteenth centuries, seismology has developed into a measurable science only in the past hundred years.

Since the late eighteenth century scientists have made a sharp distinction between volcanic and tectonic earthquakes.[8] The former were recognized as having a restricted area of impact while the latter came to be ascribed to slippages along rock surfaces (fault planes). The mechanics of this were explained by the elastic rebound theory, developed by Harry Fielding Reid after the 1906 California earthquake, which held that when the elastic strain became too great rock would rupture.[9] But as an explanation, slippage along fault planes falls into the category of immediate causation. The ultimate cause has been elusive as long as men have speculated on the origin of earthquakes. More modern explanations such as the continental drift theory, theories involving mountain building, the shrinkage of the earth's crust, the heat properties of radium, and many others have been either too restrictive, too vague, or too hypothetical.

Several public concerns converged in the 1960s in a way that focused national attention on the science of seismology. The need to detect underground nuclear explosions, concern for the safety of nuclear plants, and interest in petroleum exploration led to unprecedented financial support. This patronage has sponsored and encouraged a virtual revolution in the science. A new tectonics—the geology of the earth's structural

8. Ibid., p. 287.
9. Nicholas Hunter Heck, *Earthquakes* (New York: Hafner Publishing Co., 1965), p. 30; "Beginnings of Seismology in North America," *Earthquake Information Bulletin* 11 (March – April 1979): 47– 48.

deformations—has emerged. Verification of the sea-floor-spreading hypothesis brought new understanding of the relationship between the action of the earth's crust and earthquakes. An active global rift system, mostly on ocean floors, is now known to be a source of new surface material that moves away from rifts, eventually sinking again into the mantle beneath the crust. The strong surface layer (the lithosphere) consists of rocky plates up to fifty miles thick afloat on a partially molten layer in the mantle, which move, normally, as much as a few inches a year; these plates are bounded by the ocean ridges, island chains, and continental perimeters that constitute the great earthquake belts of the world.[10]

Earthquakes occur in these belts because two tectonic plates scrape against one another as they move. California, for instance, is an active seismic zone because it is located on the margin of the North American Plate and the East Pacific Plate, which are sliding past one another along the San Andreas fault. Earthquakes in the New Madrid region are not so neatly explained. As a general rule, the interiors of tectonic plates are relatively stable blocks where quakes may occur but less frequently than on the margins. Given the absence of obvious faults, an active region such as New Madrid is something of an anomaly. By itself such a puzzle would be enough to attract scientific interest, but obviously greater understanding of the kinds of stress responsible for the New Madrid quakes has important implications for "intra plate" quakes generally, such as those that have occasionally struck the eastern United States, particularly in determining where and under what conditions they might occur. The potentially

10. *Seismology: Responsibilities and Requirements of a Growing Science,* 2 vols. (Washington: National Academy of Sciences, 1969), for developments in the sixties.

devastating character of quakes in the New Madrid region adds an element of urgency to the search.

As early as 1912, Myron Fuller guessed that faults would be found in the primitive rock beneath the surface of the New Madrid region. Geologists have long known they must exist, but it is no simple matter to map structural deformations twenty thousand feet and more beneath the surface sediments. However, knowledge accumulated over a period of seventy years has shed a good deal of light on the question.

A Wiechert seismograph was first installed by Saint Louis University in 1909; in the eighties this had expanded to a dense network of fifty seismic stations. Seismographs make it possible to locate the source (or epicenter) of a disturbance. The location of epicenters for tremors that occurred between January 1976 and December 1978, most so minor as to be undetectable without instruments, were plotted on a map and found to form three lines. One follows a bias from southwest to northeast, intersecting another at a point a few miles south of New Madrid that moves in a north-by-northwest direction before joining a third west of New Madrid, which swerves again to the northeast. The lines zigzag from a point west of Memphis to the junction of the Ohio and Mississippi.

Discovery of a specific fault associated with the earthquakes had long remained elusive, but in the late seventies scientists of the United States Geological Survey concentrated on the lines plotted by Saint Louis University seismologists. Using a technique borrowed from the petroleum industry, they began bouncing sound waves through the crust. The result was a "picture" of the underground rock showing the characteristic vertical offsets of a fault zone that coincided with the southern branch of the line of earthquakes detected earlier by Saint Louis University seismographs.

A Question of Causation

Although, for the first time, seismicity in the region was linked to a specific geologic structure, the fault seemed too shallow to account for the deeper-seated earthquakes. However, subsequent magnetic and gravity surveys revealed the presence of a rift valley—a dropped trough in the plate rock—beneath the fault, the existence of which, like the fault, had also been inferred earlier. Rifts occur where the tectonic plate has been weakened by volcanic activity; this one was formed some five hundred million years ago. Fifty miles wide, two hundred miles in length, and twenty-five miles below the surface, this "failed" rift—a successful one would eventually have split the plate asunder— may well constitute the original geological weakness of the region. Other research has shown maximum stress to be in an east-west direction, approximately the same direction as the drift of the North American Plate. As a result, some seismologists now believe that "stress . . . is caused by drag on the bottom of the plate as it moves; earthquakes occur in the New Madrid area as drag-stress builds up and the already rifting-weakened crust gives way."[11]

One thing is certain: the periodic tremors still felt in southeastern Missouri and in surrounding states are the result of weaknesses unique to the geologic features of the region. While obviously great strides have been made toward a better understanding of these weaknesses, the possibility of a human disaster in the region remains the bottom line. More than twelve million

11. For developments in the seventies, especially the latter half: Mark Zoback, et al., "Recurrent Intraplate Tectonism in the New Madrid Seismic Zone," *Science* 209 (29 August 1980): 971–76; Robert M. Hamilton, "Quakes Along the Mississippi," *Natural History* 89 (August 1980): 70–75; an article on the earthquakes by Otto W. Nuttli, to appear in the 1981 *Yearbook of Science and Technology* (McGraw Hill). See also, *Science News.* 116 (3 November 1979): 310; 117 (5 January 1980): 9; 117 (15 June 1980): 372.

people now live in the area where damage was severe in 1811 and 1812. Certain characteristics of those earthquakes shed light on the nature of the peril and suggest what may be expected when they occur again. According to seismologist Emil J. Mateker, the "number of shocks, the continuity of the disturbance, the area affected, and severity of the sequence surpasses any recorded earthquake in the history of the North American Continent."[12] Each of these distinguishing characteristics needs to be discussed further.

Something has been said about number and continuity already, but it might be helpful at this point to recapitulate. The only dependable long-term figure came from Jared Brooks at Louisville, who counted 1,874 shocks between 16 December and 15 March. Closer to the disturbance there were attempts to keep a count, also, although none so carefully or over so extended a period. The most important was the record of William Leigh Pierce, on the Mississippi below New Madrid, who counted 89 shocks between the sixteenth and twenty-third of December. Pierce variously described 17 of these shocks as severe, very severe, long and violent, long and tremendous, long and dreadful, and great and awful. Unquestionably, if a systematic tally in the epicentral region comparable to that at Louisville had been kept, a greater number of violent shocks would have been recorded.[13]

Disturbances continued long after the period of intense activity had ended in March. Shocks were "still slightly felt . . . every 24 hours" as late as December 1812 and periodically for years thereafter. The later

12. Emil J. Mateker, "Earthquakes in Missouri," *Washington University Magazine* 39 (1968): 46. Only four million now reside in the area of most severe damage of the 1906 San Francisco quake. Nuttli, galleys, 1981 *Yearbook of Science and Technology.*

13. *New York Evening Post,* 11 February 1812.

shocks may have centered further north, in southern Illinois near Kaskaskia. Since this area had been the scene of earthquakes in 1804, it is possible that the New Madrid series triggered activity in other neighboring faults.[14]

Determining the relative severity of the New Madrid quakes raises questions of a more difficult and technical character. Seismologists agree that they had the largest magnitudes and damage areas of earthquakes that shook North America in historic time. Saint Louis University seismologist Otto W. Nuttli estimates the surface wave (often called Richter) magnitudes at 8.6, 8.4, and 8.7 for 16 December, 23 January, and 7 February respectively. The San Fernando earthquake of 1971, which killed sixty-four people, was "only" 6.6.[15] Given the absence of seismological data for the earlier series, such precise one-to-one comparisons might seem meaningless. It is at this critical juncture that historical knowledge can make a contribution. The New Madrid earthquakes went on for months and were experienced over an anomalously large land area; one consequence was a sizeable historical record made up of newspaper accounts and personal narratives. When these are compiled and set against a scale in general use today, such as the Modified Mercalli Intensity Scale, some correspondence can be achieved with modern earthquakes.

14. Zadok Cramer, *The Navigator,* 8th ed. (Pittsburgh: Cramer, Spear and Eichbaum, 1814), reprinted in Ethel C. Leahy, *Who's Who on the Ohio River and Its Tributaries* (Cincinnati: E. C. Leahy Publishing Co., 1931), p. 178; Daniel Drake, *Natural and Statistical View or Picture of Cincinnati and the Miami Country* (Cincinnati: Looker and Wallace, 1815), p. 238.

15. Hamilton, "Quakes Along the Mississippi," p. 72. Otto W. Nuttli, "Evaluation of Past Studies and Identification of Needed Studies of the Effects of Major Earthquakes Occurring in the New Madrid Fault Zone," report Submitted to Federal Emergency Management Agency, 21 January 1981, Appendix A, p. 6.

The New Madrid Earthquakes

Modified Mercalli Intensity Scale (condensed)[16]

I. Not felt except by a few under especially favorable conditions.

II. Felt only be a few persons at rest. Delicately suspended objects may swing.

III. Felt quite noticeably under favorable circumstances, but many people do not recognize seismic nature of the disturbance and many do not notice it. . . . Like passing of a truck. Duration estimated.

IV. Felt by many or most. Some awakened. Dishes, windows, doors disturbed, walls crack. Sensation like truck striking building.

V. Felt by nearly everyone; many awakened. Some dishes, windows, etc., broken; a few instances of cracked plaster; unstable objects overturned. Disturbance of trees, poles and other tall objects sometimes noticed. Pendulum clocks may stop.

VI. Felt by all; many frightened and run outdoors. Some heavy furniture moved; a few instances of fallen plaster or damaged chimneys. Damage slight.

VII. Everybody runs outdoors. Damage *negligible* in buildings of good design and construction; *slight* to moderate in well built ordinary structures; *considerable* in poorly built or badly designed structures; some chimneys broken. . . .

VIII. Damage *slight* in specially designed (brick) structures; *considerable* in ordinary substantial buildings with partial collapse; *great* in poorly built structures. Panel walls thrown out of frame structures. Fall of chimneys, factory stacks, columns, monuments, walls. Heavy furniture overturned. Sand and mud ejected in small amounts. Changes in well water. . . .

IX. Damage *considerable* in specially designed (masonry) structures; well designed frame structures thrown out of plumb; *great* in substantial (masonry) buildings, with partial collapse. Buildings shifted off foundations. Ground cracked conspicuously. Underground pipes broken.

X. Some well built wooden structures destroyed; most masonry and frame structures destroyed with foundations; ground badly cracked. . . . Landslides considerable from

16. Heck, *Earthquakes,* pp. 55–56.

river banks and steep slopes. Shifted sand and water. Water splashed (slopped) over banks.

XI. Few, if any, (masonry) structures remain standing. Bridges destroyed. Broad fissures in ground. Underground pipe lines completely out of service. Earth slumps and land slips in soft ground. . . .

XII. Damage total. Waves seen on ground surfaces. Lines of sight and level distorted. Objects thrown into the air.

Using descriptions in the published accounts of the earthquakes of 1811–1812, Nuttli constructed isoseismal maps (maps showing the range of an earthquake, divided into zones each corresponding to an assigned intensity) for the principal shocks. By correlating these maps with seismographic data from more recent earthquakes, for which intensity and area affected are known quantities, he inferred values to the ground motion, considered as a function of distance. He calculated magnitude from the values of ground motion as opposed to distance.[17] These values are achieved and expressed in a complicated mathematical terminology of interest primarily to scientists, but the intensities assigned on the isoseismal maps are quite relevant to this study, based as they are on the descriptions in the narratives as they correspond to the Modified Mercalli Intensity Scale.

Jared Brooks divided the 1,874 shocks that he counted into six classes:

First-rate, most tremendous, so as to threaten the destruction of the town, and which would soon effect it, should the action continue with the same degree of violence, buildings oscillate largely and irregularly and grind against each other, the walls split and begin to yield, chimneys, parapets, and gable ends, break in various directions and topple to the ground.

17. Otto W. Nuttli, "The Mississippi Valley Earthquakes of 1811 and 1812," *Bulletin of the Seismological Society of America* 63:1 (February 1973):228.

The New Madrid Earthquakes

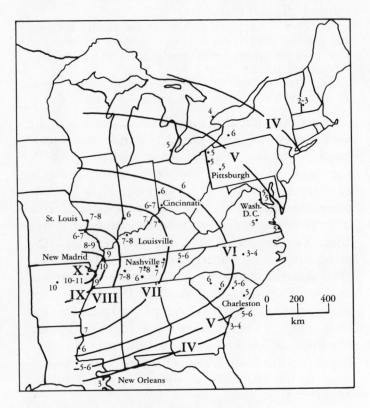

Generalized Isoseismals, 16 December 1811
Arabic numerals refer to intensities at individual points. Otto W.
Nuttli, "The Mississippi Valley Earthquakes of 1811 and 1812,"
Bulletin of the Seismological Society of America 63:1 (February
1973):230. Provided by The John Crerar Library, Chicago, Ill.
Nuttli has since revised this map. See Nuttli, "Evaluation of Past
Studies and Identification of Needed Studies of the Effects of Major
Earthquakes Occurring in the New Madrid Fault Zone," Appendix
A, p. 5. Though more complete, datum for the epicentral region is
consistent with the map shown here. However, on the new map the
area encompassed by intensity VII extends into Ohio and includes
Cincinnati.

A Question of Causation

Second rate, less violent, but severe.

Third-rate, moderate, but alarming to people generally.

Fourth-rate perceptible to the feeling of those who are still and not subject to other motion or sort of jarring that may resemble this.

[Fifth rate. Not defined.]

Sixth-rate—although often causing a strange sort of sensation, absence, and sometimes giddiness, the motion is not to be ascertained positively; but by the vibrators or other objects placed for that purpose, or accidentally.[18]

Brooks's Chart of Distribution and Intensity

End of Week	Rate						Total
	1st	2d	3d	4th	5th	6th	
22 Dec. 1811	3	2	3	1	12	66	87
29 Dec. 1811	—	—	—	—	6	150	156
5 Jan. 1812	—	1	2	9	3	119	134
12 Jan. 1812	—	1	—	10	—	150	161
19 Jan. 1812	—	—	—	4	6	55	65
26 Jan. 1812	1	1	7	2	2	78	91
2 Feb. 1812	1	—	4	6	7	191	209
9 Feb. 1812	3	5	7	5	15	140	175
16 Feb. 1812	—	—	3	6	12	65	86
23 Feb. 1812	—	—	4	6	4	278	292
1 Mar. 1812	—	—	1	4	8	126	139
8 Mar. 1812	—	—	2	9	8	39	58
15 Mar. 1812	—	—	2	3	6	210	221
Total	8	10	35	65	89	1,667	1,874

Henry McMurtrie, *Sketches of Louisville and Its Environs* (Louisville: S. Penn, 1819), p. 255.

Nuttli attempted to establish an equivalence between

18. Henry McMurtrie, *Sketches of Louisville and Its Environs* (Louisville: S. Penn, 1819), p. 255.

the Brooks classifications and the Modified Mercalli Intensity Scale:[19]

Brooks	First	Second	Third	Fourth	Fifth	Sixth
MM	VII	V– VI	IV– V	III	II	I

Most of the shocks counted by Brooks were not felt generally. One thousand six hundred and sixty seven were detected mainly on the pendulums and springs rigged by him. But Brooks was at Louisville, many miles from the epicenter.

The epicentral area for the shock of 16 December was northeastern Arkansas and a small part of southeastern Missouri. Here Nuttli estimated an intensity of X or XI. This included the part of the river on which Bradbury moored but not New Madrid or Little Prairie, and, taking the more conservative estimate, the description for intensity X seems to agree generally with the narratives: "Landslides considerable from river banks and steep slopes. Shifted sand and water. Water splashed (slopped) over banks." At New Madrid the 16 December intensity was IX, but it may have been as high as XI on 7 February. This is the difference between "damage considerable" and "few, if any," structures still standing, which, again, corresponds to the narratives. Significantly, Nuttli estimated that on 16 December the area with an intensity of VII or greater embraced 600,000 kilometers. In contrast, the area of intensity VII for the San Francisco earthquake of 1906 was no more than 30,000 kilometers. Ground movements of 16 December powerful enough to be "felt by nearly

19. Nuttli, "Mississippi Valley Earthquakes," p. 242. Daniel Drake of Cincinnati made a rudimentary classification of the principal shocks, judging their order of severity to be 7 February, 16 December, and 23 January. Drake, *Natural and Statistical View*, pp. 236– 37.

everyone" (intensity V) occurred over an area of 2,500,000 kilometers, or 965,250 square miles. Later shocks in the series could be felt over a comparable area, but otherwise no other earthquake recorded on the North American continent can approach it. Elsewhere, similar examples are extremely rare.[20]

Obviously, western shocks of equivalent power, such as the San Francisco earthquake, had a more restricted area of potential damage. In the central and eastern United States the geologic conditions of the upper ten miles of the earth's surface are such that relatively minor shocks are often felt over vast distances. In 1909 an earthquake that centered near Aurora, Illinois, forty miles west of Chicago, was felt over an area of 500,000 square miles, although damage was limited to a few collapsed chimneys in Aurora and swaying buildings in Chicago. According to Nuttli, in 1811– 1812 the "low attenuation of surface-wave energy" in eastern and central North America "produced damage and felt areas about one hundred times greater than those of western North America earthquakes of the same magnitude." Nuttli's isoseismal map for 16 December, reproduced here, is generalized, as he is careful to point out. If the lines separating the zones were drawn specifically they would show that intensities were greater in the major river valleys and areas with thick alluvial covering than in uplands and mountainous regions at similar distances from the epicenter, a fact remarked on at the time by Daniel Drake. Nor was this an unusual feature. In the great Italian earthquake at Calabria in 1783 towns on the plain had death rates that often exceeded 70 per cent, while communities in the nearby hills were immune by comparison. In 1811– 1812, what were felt as

20. Nuttli, "Mississippi Valley Earthquakes," pp. 229– 30, 232.

slight vibrations in the rock uplands were greatly magnified in the alluvial masses.[21]

The volatile surface materials found in the region of the epicenters were responsible for the great damage there. Northeastern Arkansas and southeastern Missouri are at the tip of a basin-like geologic feature known as the Mississippi Embayment. The basin is covered with a thick coating of unconsolidated alluvium and on its eastern border by deposits of loess, fine-grained dust deposited by wind.[22] The earthquakes caused extensive movement of these materials.

At distances less than 100 km, the attenuation of surface waves is controlled by geometric spreading rather than absorption, so that the attenuation of surface waves . . . in the near field region does not vary much with the surface geographic area. Thus, it is not low attenuation, but rather surficial geology which was responsible for the severity of damage in the epicentral region of the 1811 and 1812 earthquakes. There is a thick cover of alluvium, containing a layer or layers of water saturated sand, which resulted in large surface displacements, sand blows, fissures and landslides.[23]

The question of recurrence is the most intriguing (and urgent) of all. The American public is not generally aware that the five-state region below St. Louis is an active seismic zone, once the scene of a major disaster that might recur at any time. Most people realize that earthquakes occur on an infrequent and modest scale in the central and eastern United States—a few may even

21. Ibid., pp. 237, 247; Drake, *Natural and Statistical View,* p. 233; Allen Andrews, *Earthquake* (London: Angus and Robertson Ltd., 1963), p. 95; Heck, *Earthquakes,* p. 29; Myron L. Fuller, "The New Madrid Earthquake," U.S. Geological Survey *Bulletin* 494 (Washington: Government Printing Office, 1912): 32.

22. "North America's Most Violent Quake," *Natural History:* 59 (February 1950):50.

23. Nuttli, "Mississippi Valley Earthquakes," p. 245.

be aware of the disastrous Charleston earthquake of 1886—but it is San Francisco and Los Angeles, not Memphis and Cairo, that are believed to be in imminent danger of destruction.[24] Attitudes were similar in 1811. Although earthquakes were familiar enough in the eastern United States, the west was thought to be innocent of such phenomena. C. F. Volney, author of a geography published in 1804, asserted that "no trace of earthquakes" were to be found there and noted that the languages of western Indians had no word for either earthquake or volcano. Westerners knew better. Amos Stoddard contradicted Volney, enumerating several western earthquakes to set him straight.[25] Pierce found "traces of prior eruptions" and believed that the Mississippi River itself had been "formed by some great earthquake." He had no doubt that beneath its bed lay "strata upon strata of volcanic matter."

The great quantities of combustible materials, which are undoubtedly there deposited, tend to render a convulsive of this kind extremely alarming, at least, however, the beds of timber and trees interwoven and firmly matted together at the bottom of the Mississippi, are tolerable correct data from which may be presumed the prior nature &c. of the land. The trees are similar to the growth upon the banks, and why may not an inference be drawn that some tremendous agitation of nature has rent this once a continued forest, and given birth to the great and noble stream.[26]

So dramatic an origin of the Mississippi may be questionable; that prior earthquakes occurred, some of a magnitude comparable to the 1811–1812 sequence, is beyond dispute. The written record does not reveal any

24. Publicity of the discoveries of the late seventies has increased public awareness of the danger since these words were written. See "Middle America's Fault," *Time* 114 (19 November 1979): 166–67.

25. Volney, *A View of the Soil and Climate,* pp. 100–101; Stoddard, *Sketches of Louisiana,* p. 240.

26. *New York Evening Post,* 11 February 1812.

as severe, or even an alarming number. The earliest report dates from Christmas Day 1699, near the site of Memphis. John Heckewelder, the Moravian missionary, left an account of a shock felt in 1776 on the Muskingum, and others were reported in northern Kentucky in 1779 and 1792. Shocks were experienced at Kaskaskia in the Illinois country in 1795 and 1804.[27] The points of origin are not necessarily the same as in the 1811 sequence and in fact cannot be determined, but the places mentioned are all within the destructive reach of shocks originating in southeastern Missouri or northeastern Arkansas.

According to Sir Charles Lyell the Indians "had a tradition of a great earthquake which had previously devastated this same region."[28] He did not much credit the tale, but it has since been confirmed many times over by the geologic evidence. Clastic dikes—fissures of old earthquakes filled with sand—have been discovered in widely scattered localities, some of which date from Eocene and post-Eocene time. Myron Fuller found old bayous sunk by prior earthquakes with cypresses growing in them several hundred years old. At least part of the Tiptonville Dome was uplifted before 1811, and erosion of the other two domes occurred before then. Fuller also discovered cracks "as large as any of those of the last great disturbance . . . with trees fully 200 years old [growing] on their bottoms and slopes indicating early shocks of an intensity equal to if

27. Berlin Clifford Moneymaker, "Some Early Earthquakes in Tennessee and Adjacent States (1699–1850)," *Tennessee Academy of Science Journal* 29 (July 1954):227,232; Drake, *Natural and Statistical View,* pp. 243–44; Winthrop Sargent, "Account of Several Shocks of an Earthquake in the Southern and Western Parts of the United States," *Memoirs of the American Academy of Arts and Sciences 3* (1815):353–54.

28. Sir Charles Lyell, *A Second Visit to the United States of North America,* vol. 2 (New York: Harper and Brothers Publishers, 1849), p. 180.

not greater than . . . the last." More recently a trench dug athwart the fault zone has yielded evidence of at least three devastating quakes over the past two thousand years; seen in this light the 1811–1812 earthquakes are the latest examples of a long record of violent activity.[29]

The region has remained active since and continues to be highly unstable. Berlin Moneymaker cataloged many of the shocks of the nineteenth century and attempted to assign rough intensities to them based on the Modified Mercalli scale. A powerful earthquake was felt on 31 October 1895. At the epicenter near Charleston, Missouri, the intensity was IX, and intensities of III were felt in western Kansas and eastern Colorado and in the eastern seaboard states from New York to Georgia. Since 1909 the seismograph network at Saint Louis University has chronicled the continuing record; as recently as 1968 and 1976 shocks of some severity occurred. Nevertheless, if only this record were considered, the region would be of minor seismic importance. It is the great events of 1811 and 1812 and the geological evidence later unearthed as a result that leads seismologists to conclude that the region is "one of the relatively few in the United States in which there is probability" of devastatingly destructive earthquakes.[30]

29. Fuller, "New Madrid Earthquake," pp. 12–13, 73; Moneymaker, "Some Early Earthquakes," pp. 224–25; Mateker, "Earthquakes in Missouri," p. 49; George R. Mayfield, "Reelfoot Lake, the Problem Child of Tennessee," *Tennessee Academy of Science Journal* 25 (April 1950):148. Trench research is described in David P. Russ, "Late Holocene Faulting and Earthquake Recurrence in the Reelfoot Lake Area, Northwestern Tennessee," *Geological Society of America Bulletin* 90 (November 1979): 1013–18.

30. Moneymaker, "Some Early Earthquakes," pp. 224–33; "North America's Most Violent Quake," p. 50; Nuttli, "Mississippi Valley Earthquakes," p. 227; Nuttli, "Magnitude-Recurrence Rela-

The New Madrid Earthquakes

The question is not whether earthquakes will happen again in the region; clearly, they will. Rather, the question is whether they will return again in such large numbers and severity over such a long period of time. To this, of course, there is no conclusive answer. It is a historical fallacy of the first order to insist that because something has happened before it will necessarily happen again. Earthquakes do not come or stay away at the command of men; nor, so far, have they surrendered themselves to human prognostication, although earthquake prediction is nearer achievement than ever before.

On the other hand, they are the result of irreversible processes at work in the crust of the earth, the effects of which are much better understood today than once was the case. Viewed in this light the region must be eyed with considerable suspicion. The instability that resulted in the great shocks of 1811–1812 will not go away. The accumulated stresses that built up to that time were released, but there is no evidence that the adjustments were completed; far from it—the seismic activity since that time indicates a continuing instability that is less than comforting.[31]

The consequences of a return in force have haunted the region; "at St. Louis or Cincinnati, the destruction of life would be appalling," was one estimate.[32] This may seem exaggerated; after all, St. Louis, though built along the river on unconsolidated alluvium, suffered minor damage (the worst was the splitting of stone

tion for Central Mississippi Valley Earthquakes," *Bulletin of the Seismological Society of America* 64 (August 1974):1189–1207.

31. Nuttli, "Mississippi Valley Earthquakes," p. 247; Mayfield, "Reelfoot Lake," pp. 148, 155–56; Mateker, "Earthquakes in Missouri," p. 50; Fuller, "New Madrid Earthquake," p. 110.

32. John Wells Foster, *The Mississippi Valley: Its Physical Geography* (Chicago: S. C. Griggs and Co., 1869), p. 19.

houses) in 1811. But although part of the city rests on a solid base of competent rock today, many of the buildings have their foundation in clay. Tall buildings, high population density, and reliance on a much more sophisticated technology to carry out everyday activities, have made the city far more vulnerable than the frontier town of 1811.

There are other large communities close to the epicenter that did not exist in 1811. Memphis, on the fourth Chickasaw Bluff near the site of Fort Pickering, is an example. This site is only thirty-five miles from some of the largest fissures opened by the earthquakes. It experienced intensities of IX on 16 December. Referring to the description on the Modified Mercalli scale, this means, "Damage considerable in specially designed (masonry) structures; well designed frame structures thrown out of plumb; *great* in substantial (masonry) buildings, with partial collapse. Buildings shifted off foundations. Ground cracked conspicuously. Underground pipes broken." This refers to one shock, remember. To fully understand the implications, many such shocks of equal severity occurring over a period of months must be imagined. Weakened structures become increasingly susceptible to damage. Memphis today has a population of 650,000; a heavy loss of life becomes a real possibility if the earthquakes recurred on the same scale. It should be kept in mind that, because of the vast areas over which destructive shocks were felt in the central United States, the solidity of the base on which structures were built was as important as distance from the epicenter.[33] The town is both close to the origin of the disturbance and built on highly volatile materials. It is located on a loess plain atop a bluff that at water level has a layer of wet sand. Almost the same

33. Nuttli, "Mississippi Valley Earthquakes," p. 245.

conditions exist there that caused such heavy destruction at New Madrid. Cairo, Illinois, is built on a point where the Ohio meets the Mississippi. "Such points of land," according to Fuller, "were the very first to give way in the New Madrid shock and to be swallowed by the river."[34]

The people of New Madrid built again, despite the disaster of the earthquakes, a previous history of surrendering street after street to the river, and the certainty that more would be swept away in the future. Why should it have been otherwise when we know that Californians have occasionally constructed houses on the exposed outcropping of the San Andreas fault? It would be tiresome, indeed, if this book were to end on a note that served Memphis and Cairo in the shabby fashion meted out to Los Angeles, which, in a growing literature of catastrophe, has been too often allowed to slide unceremoniously into the sea. There is, wrote Louisa May Alcott in another context altogether, "a strong temptation to the weary historian to close the present tale with an earthquake which should engulf Plumfield and its environs so deeply in the bowels of the earth that no youthful Schliemann could ever find a vestige of it."[35] The novelist can give in to the temptation; the historian, weary or not, must wait for the event.

34. Fuller, "New Madrid Earthquake," p. 110; Nuttli, "Mississippi Valley Earthquakes," pp. 229, 232.
35. Louisa May Alcott, *Jo's Boys* (New York: Grosset and Dunlap, 1949), p. 358.

An Essay on Sources

The *Louisiana Gazette* (later *Missouri Gazette*) of St. Louis, the New Orleans *Louisiana Gazette and Daily Advertiser*, the *Pittsburgh Gazette*, Philadelphia *Pennsylvania Gazette, New York Evening Post, York Gazette* (of York, Upper Canada), *Quebec Mercury*, and *Montreal Herald* are important sources of information. The American papers in particular, because of their habit of reprinting accounts from a great variety of newspapers such as the Cincinnati *Western Spy* or the *Bardstown Repository*, provided a broad geographic spread. Verbatim transcripts of all material relating to the earthquakes that appeared in these newspapers from 16 December 1811 through June 1812 are available on a microfiche card attached to Otto W. Nuttli's article, "The Mississippi Valley Earthquakes of 1811 and 1812: Intensities, Ground Motion and Magnitudes," *Bulletin of the Seismological Society of America* 63 (February 1973):227–28. He used them to construct isoseismal maps as part of an important technical at tempt to establish a comparison with modern earthquakes, which is itself a pivotal source for this study.

For this purely historical reconstruction the newspapers were rich in detail and an indispensable aid in establishing chronology. Several narratives were particularly useful. The "Extract from a letter to a gentleman in Lexington, from his friend at New Madrid," which appeared in the Philadelphia *Pennsylvania Gazette*, 12 February 1812 (first published in the *Lexington Reporter*) is a unique description of the New Madrid scene on 16 and 17 December. The entry for 24 December is an account of the disaster at Little Prairie (near present-day Caruthersville). James Smith's letter

155

to Zadok Cramer, printed in the *Pittsburgh Gazette*, 13 March 1812, describes the appearance of the river after the three major shocks. There were two long narratives of experiences on the river in December by men with great powers of observation—that of John Bradbury in the 7 March issue of the St. Louis *Louisiana Gazette* and William L. Pierce in *New York Evening Post*, 11 February 1812. Pierce's narrative was printed separately as *An Account of the Great Earthquakes* (Newburyport: Herald Office, 1812); copies are rare, but one is in the Missouri Historical Society Library in St. Louis. Substantially the same account is in the appendix of Pierce's *The Year: A Poem in Three Cantoes* (New York: David Longworth, 1813). Bradbury's account is also found in Reuben Gold Thwaites, ed., *Early Western Travels, 1748–1846*, vol. 5: *Bradbury's Travels in the Interior of America, 1809–1811* (Cleveland: Arthur H. Clark Co., 1904), but the fresher newspaper narrative contains a few details that did not find their way into the later account. Without the account of Mathias Speed in the Philadelphia *Pennsylvania Gazette*, 18 March 1812, an understanding of what happened at New Madrid on 7 February would be impossible. Professor Nuttli kindly made available to me the spurious narrative of John Clarke Edwards, which did not appear on the microfiche card, with its marvelous account of volcanoes and other wonders in western North Carolina (Philadelphia *Pennsylvania Gazette*, 29 January, 19 and 26 February 1812). The letter from "A Citizen of Kentucky," *Bardstown Repository* (n.d.), in National Archives, Record Group 59, Department of State, vol. 1, "Territorial Papers, Minnesota–Missouri," p. 32, was only slightly less useful than that of Mathias Speed for the picture of the river in the vicinity of New Madrid after 7 February. A tedious but useful condensation of newspaper accounts is Samuel Latham Mitchill's "A

Detailed Narrative of the Earthquakes Which Occurred on the Sixteenth Day of December, 1811, and Agitated the Parts of North America That Lie between the Atlantic Ocean and Louisiana; and Also a Particular Account of the Other Quakings of the Earth Occasionally Felt from That Time to the Twenty-third and Thirtieth of January, and the Seventh and Sixteenth of February, 1812, and Subsequently to the Eighteenth of December, 1813, and Which Shook the Country from Detroit and the Lakes to New Orleans and the Gulf of Mexico," which appeared in the *Transactions of the Literary and Philosophical Society of New York* 1 (1814):281–307.

The "New Madrid Extract" is valuable particularly because other accounts of events in the town were written from memory years later. The account of Col. John Shaw appeared in the second annual report and collections of the State Historical Society of Wisconsin for 1855, later printed ("New Madrid Earthquake: Account of Colonel John Shaw") in the *Missouri Historical Review* 6 (1912):91–92; the account of Timothy Dudley ("The Earthquake of 1811 at New Madrid, Missouri [from the Narrative of an Eyewitness]") in the *Annual Report of the Board of Regents of the Smithsonian Institution Showing the Operations, Expenditures, and Condition of the Institution for the Year 1858* (Washington, 1859), pp. 421–24, was based on the eyewitness narration of James Ritchie of Jerseyville, Illinois, who resided in the New Madrid district during the earthquakes. Vincent Nolte's account appeared in his memoirs, *Fifty Years in Both Hemispheres* (London: Trubner and Co., 1854). All three contain good descriptions of 7 February. Among sources most often quoted is Eliza Bryan's letter, which appeared in *The History of Cosmopolite; or, the Four Volumes of Lorenzo Dow's Journal* (Wheeling, Va.: Joshua Martin, 1848). Equally popular has been the account of

Godfrey Lesieur (or LeSieur), which can be found many places; see, for instance, Robert A. Campbell, ed., *Campbell's Gazetteer of Missouri; from Articles Contributed by Prominent Gentlemen in Each County of the State, and Information Collected and Collated from Official Sources, by a Corps of Experienced Canvassers* (St. Louis: R. A. Campbell, 1874), and W. F. Switzler, *Switzler's Illustrated History of Missouri from 1541 to 1877* (St. Louis: C. R. Burns, 1879). Other material by Lesieur is in Daughters of the American Revolution, Lucy Jefferson Lewis Chapter (New Madrid), "New Madrid Earthquakes, 1811– 12, compiled from the New Madrid archive in New Madrid county courthouse," manuscript in Missouri Historical Society Library, St. Louis, Mo. A somewhat later account, based on Lesieur, is Lewis F. Linn's letter in Alphonso Wetmore's *Gazetteer of the State of Missouri* (St. Louis: C. Keemle, 1837). The emotional response to the desolation of a ruined village is described vividly in the account of James McBride, "Brief Accounts of Journies in the Western Country, 1809– 1812," which appeared in the *Quarterly Publication of the Historical and Philosophical Society of Ohio* 5 (January– March 1910):27– 31.

Several other narratives by persons located at various points in the area of principal disturbance were useful. First among these was the account of Louis Bringier, "Notices of the Geology, Mineralogy, Topography, Production, and Aboriginal Inhabitants of the Regions around the Mississippi and Its Confluent Waters," which appeared in the *American Journal of Science and Arts 3* (1821):15– 46. John James Audubon's experiences in Kentucky were related in *Audubon and His Journals* (New York: Charles Scribner's Sons, 1897), edited by Maria R. Audubon. Another Kentucky description was that of William Brown. An extract from his journal was published in *Science* 71 (14 March

An Essay on Sources

1930):285–86 by his great-grandson, William Allen Pusey. *A Journal of Two Campaigns of the Fourth Regiment of U.S. Infantry, in the Michigan and Indiana Territories . . . during the Years 1811 and 1812* (Keene, N. H.: Printed by the author, 1816) was by Adam Walker, a trooper in Harrison's campaign against Tecumseh and the Prophet who was in Vincennes recovering from a wound received at Tippecanoe when the first shocks struck. A number of narratives and useful references to the earthquakes were found in Clarence Edwin Carter, ed., *Territorial Papers of the United States*, vol. 14: *Louisiana–Missouri, 1806–1814* (Washington: Government Printing Office, 1949).

Outside the area of principal disturbance the most important source was the detailed record of Jared Brooks, which appeared as an appendix of Henry McMurtrie, *Sketches of Louisville and Its Environs* (Louisville: S. Penn, 1819). Only slightly less useful was the account by Daniel Drake in his *Natural and Statistical View or Picture of Cincinnati and the Miami Country* (Cincinnati: Looker and Wallace, 1815), and that of Winthrop Sargent of Natchez, "Account of Several Shocks of an Earthquake in the Southern and Western Parts of the United States," in the *Memoirs of the American Academy of Arts and Sciences* 3 (1815):350–60. Portions of the Brooks record also appeared in Benjamin Casseday's *The History of Louisville from Its Earliest Settlement till the Year 1852* (Louisville: Hull and Brothers, 1852). Of somewhat lesser interest is Edward Darrell Smith, "On the Changes Which Have Taken Place in the Wells Situated in Columbia, S.C. Since the Earthquakes of 1811–12," in the *American Journal of Science and Arts* 1:1 (1818):93–95.

A number of persons investigated the scene, interviewed eyewitnesses, and left accounts. Timothy Flint's *Recollections of the Last Ten Years* (New York:

Alfred A. Knopf, 1932), first published in Boston, in 1826, is probably the most widely quoted. A biography of the versatile Flint is John Ervin Kirkpatrick's *Timothy Flint, Pioneer, Missionary, Author, Editor, 1780–1840* (Cleveland: Arthur H. Clark Co., 1911). Three scientists left accounts. Edwin James, *Account of an Expedition from Pittsburgh to the Rocky Mountains under the Command of Major Stephen H. Long,* 2 vols. (Ann Arbor: University Microfilms, 1966) not only described later shocks at Cape Girardeau but also relates an interesting legend among the Otoes. Thomas Nuttall accompanied John Bradbury on his voyage up the Missouri in 1810 but was not with him on his return down the Mississippi. In 1818 he returned to the scene of his friend's encounter with the earthquakes and described this visit in *A Journal of Travels into the Arkansa Territory*, vol. 63 (Ann Arbor: University Microfilms, 1966). Sir Charles Lyell left a graphic description of the sunken country in *A Second Visit to the United States of North America*, 2 vols. (New York: Harper and Brothers Publishers, 1849). Samuel M. McDaniel recorded the recollections of his grandfather in "Journals and Diaries," manuscript in the Missouri Historical Society archive, St. Louis, Mo.

To supplement the newspaper narratives of events on the river Zadok Cramer's *The Navigator, Containing Directions for Navigating the Monongahela, Allegheny, Ohio and Mississippi Rivers* was essential. The eighth edition (Pittsburgh: Cramer, Spear and Eichbaum, 1814) was used here. No one took to the river without a copy. Often revised, it numbered all the islands and bars; described the channel, banks, towns, and settlements in great detail; incorporated relevant correspondence and other miscellany useful to boatmen (and inquisitive historians); and gave accurate mileages from the mouth of the Ohio. Very little is known of Cramer, but by his own testimony he was a boy in "the Pines, of New Jersey." The eighth edition, the first after the earthquakes, appeared in Ethel C. Leahy, *Who's Who on the Ohio River and Its Tributaries* (Cincinnati: E. C. Leahy Publishing Co., 1931), itself a mine of detail, trivial and otherwise. Also relevant to changes on the river was F. C. Usher, "On the Elevation of the Banks of the Mississippi in 1811," in the *American Journal of Science and Arts* 31 (1837):294–96.

In addition to newspapers and other sources three accounts were useful in reconstructing the voyage of the *New Orleans.* The standard work is Louis C. Hunter and Beatrice Jones Hunter, *Steamboats on the Western Rivers: An Economic and Technological History* (Cambridge: Harvard University Press, 1949), which is good on background but without much to say about the voyage itself. For that one must turn to Charles Joseph Latrobe, *The Rambler in North America,* 2 vols. (London: R. B. Seeley and W. Burnside, 1835) and J. H. B. Latrobe, *The First Steamboat Voyage on the Western Waters* (Baltimore: John Murphy, Printer, 1871), the latter Lydia Roosevelt's brother. These accounts differ significantly in several details, and of the two that of J. H. B. Latrobe seems from internal evidence the more reliable; he at least clearly had access to family papers as well as the reminiscences of Lydia Latrobe. Charles Joseph Latrobe preserved the apparently apochryphal story of the migrating squirrels. This colorful tale has fascinated other historians of the earthquakes. Margaret Ross, "The New Madrid Earthquake," *Arkansas Historical Quarterly* 27 (Summer 1968):83–104, in an otherwise generally reliable article, accepted it uncritically. Since it cannot be corroborated, the mass migration of the small, furry quadrupeds invites skepticism.

Some of these sources—mainly Bryan, Lesieur,

Bringier, Brooks, Drake, Flint, and Nuttall—have been quoted extensively along with other related material in a variety of works. A list, in alphabetical order, of the most useful follows: Lewis C. Beck, *Gazetteer of the States of Illinois and Missouri* (Albany, N.Y.: Lewis Cable Beck, 1823); G. C. Broadhead, "The New|Madrid Earthquake," *American Geologist* 30 (1902):76–87; John Wells Foster, *The Mississippi Valley: Its Physical Geography* (Chicago: S. C. Griggs and Co., 1869); *History of Southeast Missouri* (Chicago: Goodspeed Publishing Co., 1888); Murat Halstead, *The World on Fire, Including Splendors and Horrors of the Volcanic Eruptions of the Lesser Antilles, Together with a Biographical Sketch of Josephine, Empress of the French, the Fair Daugher of Martinique, and Alexander Hamilton, Stalwart Son of the Island of Nevis and Father of the American Constitution* (New York: International Publishing Co., 1902); John Haywood, *The Natural and Aboriginal History of Tennessee Up to the First Settlement Therein by the White People, in the Year 1768* (Nashville: George Wilson, 1823); Samuel Prescott Hildreth, "History of a Voyage from Marietta to New Orleans in 1805 (Chap. 5, from the Mouth of the Ohio to Fort Pickering)," *The American Pioneer* 1 (1842):128–45; Henry Howe, *Historical Collections of the Great West, Containing Narratives of the Most Important and Interesting Events in Western History,* 2 vols. (Cincinnati: Henry Howe, 1851); James T. Lloyd, *Lloyd's Steamboat Directory and Disasters on the Western Waters* (Cincinnati: J. T. Lloyd and Co., 1856); William S. Mosely, "New Madrid, Missouri," *Western Journal* 3 (March 1850):385–90; James Handasyd Perkins, *Annals of the West: Embracing a Concise Account of the Principal Events, Which Have Occurred in the Western States and Territories, from the Discovery of the Mississippi Valley to the Year Eighteen*

An Essay on Sources

Hundred and Forty-six, Compiled from the Most Authentic Sources (Cincinnati: J. R. Albach, 1846).

Several works not themselves concerned with the earthquakes were helpful. Estwick Evans, *A Pedestrious Tour, of Four Thousand Miles, through the Western States and Territories during the Winter and Spring of 1818* (Concord, N.H.: Joseph C. Spear, 1819), is full of colorful details of the experience of flatboating on the river. D. T. Madox, *Late Account of the Missouri Territory* (Paris, Ky.: John Lyle, 1817) covers some of the same ground as Henry Brackenridge, in language suspiciously similar. Timothy Flint's work, *The History and Geography of the Mississippi Valley; to Which Is Appended a Condensed Physical Geography of the Atlantic United States, and the Whole American Continent,* 2 vols. (Cincinnati: E. H. Flint and L. R. Lincoln, 1832) has useful detail of the region's development after the earthquakes. Not itself concerned with the Mississippi Valley, C. F. Volney's *A View of the Soil and Climate of the United States of America* (Philadelphia: J. Conrad and Co., 1804), has much to say of the earthquake history of eastern America and of the absence of earthquakes in the west—a contention that enraged Stoddard. Volney's source for earthquake matters was Samuel Williams, *The Natural and Civil History of Vermont* (Walpole, N.H., 1794).

The eschatological response to the earthquakes was pieced together from a variety of works. References to the comet are found scattered through the narratives. Two scientists made useful observations; both, by John Farrar ("Observations of the Comet of 1811") and Nathaniel Bowditch ("Elements of the Orbit of the Comet of 1811"), appeared in the *Memoirs of the American Academy of Arts and Sciences* 3 (1815):308–26. Earthquakes elsewhere aroused much anxiety. The most disastrous, that at Caracas, is discussed in E. Taylor Parks, "Foreign Aid—150 Years Ago," *Foreign Service Journal* 39:7 (July 1962): 36–39. The *Autobiography of Rev. James B. Finley; or, Pioneer Life in the West,* W. P. Strickland, ed. (Cincinnati: Methodist Book Concern, 1854), has useful and colorful details of the impact on religion, and Walter Brownlow Posey, "The Earthquake of 1811 and Its Influence on Evangelistic Methods in the Churches of the Old South," *Tennessee Historical Magazine* 1:2 (1931):107–14, draws some interesting conclusions. Henry Rowe Schoolcraft, *Transallegania; or, the Groans of Missouri* (New York: J. Seymour, Printer, 1820), makes use of the theme of retribution, and Harry Harrison Kroll's historical romance, *Fury in the Earth: A Novel of the New Madrid Earthquakes* (Indianapolis: Bobbs-Merrill Co., 1945), emphasizes the religious experience of the earthquakes. Schoolcraft's poem appears as an appendix to some editions of his *Journal of a Tour into the Interior of Missouri and Arkansas, from Potosi, or Mine à Burton, in Missouri Territory, in a Southwest Direction, toward the Rocky Mountains; Performed in the Years 1818 and 1819* (London: Sir Richard Phillips and Co., 1821). A biography of Schoolcraft is Chase S. Osborn and Stellanova Osborn, *Schoolcraft, Longfellow, Hiawatha* (Lancaster, Pa.: Jaques Cattell Press, 1942). Two other novels using the earthquake are Dale Van Every, *The Trembling Earth* (New York: Julian Messner, 1953) and Janice Holt Giles, *The Believers* (Boston: Houghton Mifflin Co., 1957).

While speaking of fiction, one should mention *Fagots from the Campfire* (Washington: E. T. Charles & Co., 1881) by "The Newspaper Man" (Louis J. Dupré), which, while set in a later era, contains many fanciful recollections of the earthquakes. It also asserts that the people in the vicinity of Union City, Tennessee, feared that their town was built on the roof of an underground cavern similar to the one believed to have collapsed in the creation of Reelfoot—apparently a widespread popular belief at the time James MacFarlane insisted the earthquakes were not earthquakes at all but the result of subsidence (in "The 'Earthquake' at New Madrid, Missouri, in 1811, Probably Not an Earthquake," *Proceedings of the American Association for the Advancement of Science* 32 [August 1883]:247–48).

Material on Indians is also scattered through the narratives, but several works were particularly useful. *Tecumseh: Vision of Glory* (New York: Bobbs-Merrill Co., 1956) by Glenn Tucker is the best modern biography. Benjamin Drake, *Life of Tecumseh* (Cincinnati: Queen City Publishing House, 1852) is the older study. James Mooney's study of "The Ghost-Dance Religion and the Sioux Outbreak of 1890" and its relation to earlier religious revivals, such as the Prophet's, is found in *Fourteenth Annual Report of the Bureau of American Ethnology for 1892–93* 14:2 (Washington: Government Printing Office, 1896): 665–78. John Dunn Hunter's memory of Tecumseh's words to the Osage after the earthquakes is in his *Memoirs of a Captivity Among the Indians of North America* (New York: Schocken Books, 1973), edited by Richard Drinnon. No fair-minded reader of Drinnon's *White Savage* (New York: Schocken Books, 1972) can any longer maintain that Hunter was an impostor and his book a hoax. The Indian legend of the origin of Reelfoot is in Federal Writer's Project, *Tennessee: A Guide to the State* (New York: Viking Press, 1939).

The great influence of electricity is discussed in several basic sources: I. Bernard Cohen, ed., *Benjamin Franklin's Experiments: A New Edition of Franklin's Experiments and Observations on Electricity* (Cambridge: Harvard University Press, 1941); Stephen F. Mason, *A*

History of the Sciences (New York: Collier Books, 1962); Philip C. Ritterbush, *Overtures to Biology: The Speculations of Eighteenth-Century Naturalists* (New Haven: Yale University Press, 1964); A. Wolf, *A History of Science, Technology, and Philosophy in the Eighteenth Century* (London: George Allen and Unwin Ltd., 1952). *Encyclopaedia; or, a Dictionary of Arts, Sciences, and Miscellaneous Literature; Constructed on a Plan, by Which the Different Sciences and Arts Are Digested into the Form of Distinct Treatises of Systems . . . The First American Edition, in Eighteen Volumes, Greatly Improved,* vol. 6 (Philadelphia: Thomas Dobson, Printer, 1798), otherwise known as *Britannica,* the third edition, pp. 264–88, 535–39, has the best contemporary summary.

For the evolution of seismology as a science, see James Dewey and Perry Byerly, "The Early History of Seismometry (to 1906)," *Bulletin of the Seismological Society of America* 59 (1969): 183–227. For recent developments, see *Seismology: Responsibilities and Requirements of a Growing Science,* 2 vols. (Washington: National Academy of Sciences, 1969). *The Earthquake History of the United States* (Washington: Government Printing Office, 1973) is covered by Jerry L. Coffman and Carl A. von Hake, editors. A more general history is *Great Earthquakes* (London: Thomas Murby and Co., 1936) by Charles Davison. Nicholas Hunter Heck, *Earthquakes* (New York: Hafner Publishing Co., 1965), C. F. Richter, *Elementary Seismology* (San Francisco: W. H. Freeman Co., 1958), and Allen Andrews, *Earthquake* (London: Angus and Robertson, Ltd., 1963), are good general summaries.

There are several earlier reconstructions, both historical and scientific, of the earthquakes. The most complete is Myron Fuller's "The New Madrid Earthquake" in U.S. Geological Survey *Bulletin* 494 (Washington: Government Printing Office, 1912).

An Essay on Sources

Some of Fuller's other writings are also of interest, especially "Earthquakes and the Forest" in *Forestry and Irrigation* 12 (1906):261–67 and "Our Greatest Earthquakes," *Popular Science Monthly* 69 (July 1906):|76–86. An earlier survey is Nathaniel Southgate Shaler, "Earthquakes of the Western United States," *Atlantic Monthly* 24:145 (November 1869):549–59. More complete is Berlin Clifford Moneymaker, "Some Early earthquakes in Tennessee and Adjacent States (1699–1850)," *Tennessee Academy of Science Journal* 29 (July 1954):224–33. Shaler also covers the subject briefly in *Kentucky* (Boston: Houghton Mifflin and Co., 1884). E. M. Shepard, "The New Madrid Earthquake," *Journal of Geology* 13 (1905):45–62, should be read with MacFarlane. W J McGee, "A Fossil Earthquake," *Bulletin of the Geological Society of America* 4 (28 December 1892):411–14, is very useful if read critically. Emil J. Mateker, "Earthquakes in Missouri," *Washington University Magazine* 39 (1968):46–51, should be read with Nuttli. Of more topical interest is William Clifford Morse, "New Madrid Earthquake Craters," *Bulletin of the Seismological Society of America* 31 (1941):309–19. Alexander von Humboldt discusses the earthquakes in *Cosmos,* 5 vols. (London: H. G. Bohm, 1849). Reelfoot Lake is taken up in David Dale Owen, *Report of the Geological Survey in Kentucky, Made during the Years 1854 and 1855,* 4 vols. (Frankfort, Ky.: A. G. Hodges, Printer, 1856–1861), and George R. Mayfield, "Reelfoot Lake, the Problem Child of Tennessee," *Tennessee Academy of Sciences Journal* 25 (April 1950):148–56. "Reelfoot–a Strange Spot," in *American Forests* 59 (1953):26–27, by Sidney Snook, is brief and impressionistic. A fossil skull ejected by an earthquake eruption is described by J. E. DeKay in "Notes on a Fossil Skull in the Cabinet of the Lyceum, of the Genus Bos, from the Banks of the Mississippi; with Observations on the American Species of That Genus," New York Academy of Sciences, *Annals of the Lyceum of Natural History* 2 (March 1826):280–91.

Recent developments can be followed in a number of technical articles, though they may be daunting to those not of a seismological persuasion. Mark Zoback, et al., "Recurrent Intraplate Tectonism in the New Madrid Seismic Zone," *Science* 209 (29 August 1980): 971–76, is the place to begin. Other useful discussions are C. Patrick Ervin and L. D. McGinnis, "Reelfoot Rift: Reactivated Precursor to the Mississippi Embayment," *Bulletin of the Geological Society of America* 86 (September 1975): 1287–95; Robert B. Herrman, et al., "Archeoseismology Applied to the New Madrid Earthquakes of 1811 to 1812," *Bulletin of the Seismological Society of America* 68 (1978): 1751–59; William Stauder, S. J., "Microearthquake Array Studies of the Seismicity in Southeast Missouri," *Earthquake Information Bulletin* 8 (January–February 1977): 8–13; and William Stauder et al., "Seismic Characteristics of Southeast Missouri as Indicated by a Regional Microearthquake Array," *Bulletin of the Seismological Society of America* 66 (1976): 1953–64; Dennis O'Leary, "Remote Sensing for Lineaments in the Mississippi Embayment," *Earthquake Information Bulletin* 9 (January–February 1977): 14–18. Of special interest is Otto W. Nuttli's "Evaluation of Past Studies and Identification of Needed Studies of the Effects of Major Earthquakes Occurring in the New Madrid Fault Zone," a report submitted to Federal Emergency Management Agency, 21 January 1981. See also "The Evaluation of Earthquake Hazard in the Central Mississippi Valley," *American Nuclear Society Transactions* 26 (1977): 126 by the same author. Robert M. Hamilton has written a summary easily comprehensible to the layman of the state of seismological knowledge in the New Madrid region: "Quakes along the Mississippi," *Natural History* 89 (August 1980): 70–75.

Wayne Viitanen has written extensively on the earthquakes; see his doctoral dissertation, "The Winter the Mississippi Ran Backwards: The Impact of the New Madrid Earthquake of 1811–1812 on Life and Letters in the Mississippi Valley," Southern Illinois University, 1972; also "Folklore and Fakelore of an Earthquake," *Kentucky Folklore Record* 19 (1973): 99–111, and "The Winter the Mississippi Ran Backwards: Early Kentuckians Report the New Madrid, Missouri, Earthquake of 1811–1812," *Register of the Kentucky Historical Society* 71 (January 1973):51–68. "Popular Reactions to the New Madrid Earthquakes, 1811–1812," is in *Filson Club History Quarterly* 50 (January 1976): 60–71, by Marshall Scott Legan. A popular treatment is "America's Greatest Earthquake," *Reader's Digest* 94 (April 1969): 110–14, by B. Clark. An earlier study is Francis A. Sampson, "The New Madrid and Other Earthquakes in Missouri," *Mississippi Valley Historical Association Proceedings* 6 (1913):218–38. This article proliferated in other places; see *Bulletin of the Seismological Society of America* 3 (1913):57–71 and *Missouri Historical Review* 7 (1913):179–99. Raymond Spears, "The New Madrid Earthquake Country," *Americana* 5 (1910):326–32, has some useful references.

The origin of New Madrid has been studied by Max Savelle in *George Morgan: Colony Builder* (New York: Columbia University Press, 1932) and "The Founding of New Madrid, Missouri," *Mississippi Valley Historical Review* 19 (1932):30–56. See also Floyd C. Shoemaker, "New Madrid, Mother of Southeast Missouri," *Missouri Historical Review* 49 (1955): 317–27. Also useful were James Ripley Jacobs, *Tarnished Warrior: Major-General James Wilkinson* (New York: Macmillan Co., 1938), James Alton James, *The Life of George Rogers*

The New Madrid Earthquakes

Clark (Chicago: University of Chicago Press, 1928), and Gaillard Hunt, ed., *The Writings of James Madison,* vol. 5 (New York: G. P. Putnam's Sons, 1904). Glimpses of New Madrid before the earthquakes are found in Georges Henri Victor Collot, *A Journey in North America* (Paris: Printed for Arthus Bertrand, Bookseller, 1826); Francis Baily, *Journal of a Tour in Unsettled Parts of North America in 1796 and 1797* (London: Baily Brothers, 1856); Thomas Ashe, *Travels in America, Performed in the Year 1806 for the Purpose of Exploring the Rivers Alleghany, Monongahela, Ohio, and the Mississippi, and Ascertaining the Produce and Condition of the Banks and Vicinity* (London: Printed for Richard Phillips, 1809); Amos Stoddard, *Sketches, Historical and Descriptive, of Louisiana* (Philadelphia: Mathew Carey, 1812); and Henry Marie Brackenridge, *Views of Louisiana: Together with a Journal of a Voyage up the Missouri River, in 1811* (Pittsburgh: Cramer, Spear and Eichbaum, 1814). In addition to Edwin James, Flint, Nuttall, and Lyell, William Darby, *The Emigrant's Guide* (New York: Kirk and Merclin, 1818), and Samuel R. Brown, *The Western Gazetteer; or, Emigrant's Directory; Containing a Geographical Description of the Western States and Territories* (Auburn, N.Y.: H. C. Southwick, 1817), were helpful in getting a view of the town after the earthquakes. So was Edouard de Montulé, *Travels in America, 1816–1817;* translated from the original French edition of 1821 by Edward D. Sieber (Bloomington: Indiana University Press, 1950). John Reps, "New Madrid on the Mississippi," Society of Architectural Historians *Journal* 18 (March 1959): 21–26, discusses the annual collapse of the banks and the deterioration of the site. See also his *Town Planning in Frontier America* (reprint by the University of Missouri Press, 1980).

A number of Missouri studies deserve mention. On

the natural history of the state I found C. F. Marbut, "The Evolution of the Northern Part of the Lowlands of Southeastern Missouri," in the *University of Missouri Studies* 1 (July 1902):1– 63, the most helpful. Somewhat dated, but still useful, is James Fernando Ellis, *The Influence of Environment on the Settlement of Missouri* (St. Louis: Webster Publishing Co., 1929). Louis Houck, *A History of Missouri from the Earliest Exploration and Settlement until the Admission of the State into the Union,* 3 vols. (reprint by Arno Press and *New York Times,* 1971), is still definitive in many ways. His *The Spanish Régimé in Missouri,* 2 vols. (Chicago: R. R. Donnelly and Sons, 1909), has most of the documents on the Morgan episode in New Madrid's history. "A Letter from New Madrid," edited by E. G. Swem, in *Mississippi Valley Historical Review* 5 (1918):342– 46, was also useful in this regard. Three other state histories were helpful—Lucien Carr, *American Commonwealths: Missouri a Bone of Contention* (Boston and New York: Houghton Mifflin Co., Edwin 1888), McReynolds, *Missouri: A History of the Crossroads State* (Norman: University of Oklahoma Press, 1962); a very readable recent contribution is the first volume of the Missouri Sesquicentennial Edition under the general editorship of William E. Parrish, *A History of Missouri,* vol. 1: *1673 to 1820* (Columbia: University of Missouri Press, 1971), by William E. Foley. Those who like their history in verse are invited to look at Jasamyn Sanders Garrett, *Bountiful Bootheel Borning: A History in Narrative Verse* (Hayté, Mo.: the author, 1961). Though elderly now, *The Literature of the Middle Western Frontier,* 2 vols. (New York: Columbia University Press, 1926), by Ralph Rusk, is still an indispensable bibliography. Also useful was Brenda Elizabeth Richard, *Index to the New Madrid Archive, 1791– 1804* (St. Louis, 1940) in the Missouri Historical Society Library, St. Louis.

Index

Index

Index

Index